Peter Lewis is the pseudonym of a leading West End solicitor, and David Lewis, psychologist and author of more than twenty best-selling books. They have previously written two serious legal books, *Most Unnatural – an Enquiry into the Stafford Case* and *Just How Just*, still a standard text on many law courses.

By the same author

*Most Unnatural – an Enquiry into
   the Stafford Case*
Just How Just

PETER LEWIS

Brief Encounters

Illustrated by McLachlan

GRAFTON BOOKS

A Division of the Collins Publishing Group

LONDON GLASGOW
TORONTO SYDNEY AUCKLAND

Grafton Books
A Division of the Collins Publishing Group
8 Grafton Street, London W1X 3LA

A Grafton Paperback Original 1989

A CIP catalogue record for this book is available
from the British Library

ISBN 0-586-20454-7

Printed and bound by
Collins, Glasgow

Set in Janson

Introduction

During the trial of Mrs Cynthia Payne, who had been charged with controlling prostitutes, Judge Brian Pryor cautioned the jury that the trial was 'not a form of entertainment'. Here he was badly mistaken. While the drama being enacted ranges from farce to tragedy, depending on the role in which you have been cast, the law has clearly long been a branch of show business.

Why else would mature and intelligent professionals don wigs and knee-breeches, put on crimson robes and indulge in dialogue as arcane and obscure as that of a Japanese Noh Play?

Why else would the public queue for hours to get a seat in the gallery when an especially juicy drama is being played out?

Why else should the criminal trial have, for so long, attracted playwrights and novelists?

In this guide to the law I shall be exploring the various roles available – from burglars to barristers and detectives to defendants – to discover how to avoid bad notices and enjoy rave reviews in this fascinating branch of show business.

We'll start by considering those players on whose tireless endeavours the incomes of so many honourable citizens depend – the criminals.

ONE

Opportunities in Crime

'I think crime pays. The hours are good and you travel a lot.'

Woody Allen – *Take the Money and Run*

For rave notices and a long run – in fact the further the better – your role must be bold and daring. If it is played with sufficient drama you could become an instant celebrity. Chat show hosts, tabloid journalists, and film directors – not to mention your sternest critics, the police – will be beating a path to your cell door. Middle-aged pop stars could be begging for the chance to re-create your original role.

Training

Although the criminal performance must be learned mainly on the job, the government has established a number of residential training schools – more commonly referred to as prisons – for aspiring criminals of all ages. They offer free lodging and specialist tuition from experts in their fields. Apply through the courts.

Prospects

While I would in no way wish to encourage or condone this branch of the business, it has to be admitted that for those with superstar status the financial returns can prove attractive.

Unfortunately, being a star means high living expenses as you flaunt your success before an admiring public. A typical evening will include cocktails at the Inter-Continental, dinner at Langan's, a table at Tramp, half a dozen magnums of Moët, and five or six grams of the best Bolivian. All this means that even a modest lifestyle requires an income of at least £3,000 per week.

As with any star, major expenses are clothes, fast cars, large houses, lavish gifts for friends and private schooling for your children.

What role should you choose?

Not long ago armed robbery offered the most exciting opportunities for glamour, drama and reward. Today it has fallen out of favour. Heavy traffic and the clamp make quick getaways problematic. Banks keep their money in vaults rather than in easily accessible piles behind the counter. You have to kidnap the bank manager at home and put up with his dreadful flocked wallpaper and dreary suburban conversation while waiting anything up to twelve hours for the time locks to open.

On the plus side you'll get invited to some of the best West End parties, be treated with great deference at London clubs, and enjoy respect should you be careless enough to get jailed. There is also enhanced physical allure. Some women find armed robbery sexually arousing.

Learning The Language

Should you decide to embark on a career in crime, a basic grasp of the jargon will prove a distinct advantage. Without it leading West End lawyers may refuse to believe you are a superstar and refuse to act as your agents. Here's a basic vocabulary to get started.

Blag	robbery (verb to blag) as in: 'I done a blagging'
Boob	prison
Dipper	pickpocket
Drugs	Charlie is cocaine; Smack is heroin; Bob

	Hope is dope (Black = Afghan; Red = Lebanese; Rock and Roll = Moroccan); Speed is amphetamine sulphate
Flop	safe house for use before and after robbery
Hoisting	shop-lifting
Kite	cheque, hence kiting – passing dud cheques
Loid	piece of plastic for slipping Yale locks
Money	Bull's eye – £5
	Pony – £25
	Long 'un – £100
	Monkey – £500
On the creep	a walk-in burglary, of offices, etc
On the jump up	Stealing goods from lorries
Ringer	stolen car whose number plates have been changed
Ringing the changes	cheating shopkeepers out of change
Slaughter	hiding place for stolen goods
Snides	forgeries, usually

	currency or counterfeit goods
Tool	gun, weapons in general, viz 'going on a blag tooled up'

How To Succeed In Crime

START YOUNG

Arrested for picking the pocket of Santa Claus in a New York department store, twelve-year-old Art Drunker stole and ate the officer's sandwiches while being driven to the police station. 'He's a swell kid who should go far,' commented the arresting officer.

*   *

Miss Mae Wakko, aged fifteen, the daughter of a religious novelties salesman from Tulsa, admitted that she had, throughout the summer, withdrawn the whole of her parents' life savings by forging their signatures on with-drawal slips. She used the money to buy two Thunderbirds, a Jaguar, a Lincoln Continental, 450 cases of champagne and several strings of European pearls. Her lawyer, Mr Waddy Bernstein, told the court: 'She's a good girl who only did it to bring happiness to others.'

*   *

Ten-year-old Amilio DeMillo, arrested on shop-lifting charges in a Los Angeles department store, was being hunted by police after stealing the patrol car in which he was about to be taken to the station. 'He's a son-of-a-bitch who's gone too far,' said a police spokesman.

PLAN CAREFULLY

Soon after the M1 was opened, four South London burglars decided the motorway offered a convenient way to rob offices in Luton. One which attracted their attention was said to hold £25,000 of wages in its safe. Leaving Dartford around ten-thirty one night, three of the gang drove to the home of the fourth, their explosives specialist. Finding he was still out at the pub they decided to proceed without him.

When they arrived at Luton they successfully broke into the office only to find the safe beyond their meagre skills. They drove back to Dartford.

With difficulty they awoke the expert and drove him to Luton. After inspecting the job he announced that more explosives than he had with him would be needed. These were in his shed at home. They drove back to Dartford.

Having collected more plastic explosive they returned to Luton. The safe was blown. Unfortunately their man had used insufficient explosive and the door jammed halfway. A crowbar was needed to force it open. The crowbar was at the explosives expert's home. They drove back to Dartford.

Collecting the crowbar they made their fourth trip of the night to Luton. With much effort they prised open the safe. It contained £2 26p. By now it was almost dawn. They drove back to Dartford.

At the end of the motorway they were stopped by a random police check. In the boot of their car, patrol officers found masks, office-breaking equipment, a crowbar and lots of gelignite.

'Try pleading insanity,' suggested their solicitor.

*   *

Sean Logan and Patrick Horsferry decided to break into a Belfast supermarket via the offices above. Entering the premises one Saturday night they started cutting their way through the flooring. A short while later it collapsed abruptly, dropping both men through the floor and on to the pavement below, almost at the feet of a startled policeman. In their enthusiasm they had failed to notice they were cutting through a part of the floor which overhung the road-way by some fifteen feet.

*   *

Failing to open a ten-cwt safe located on the top floor of a twelve-storey office block, Don Fortune, twenty-two, and James Riddle, forty-six, decided to remove it to their own premises where they might work on the locks at leisure.

With difficulty they dragged the safe to the steep flight of wooden stairs.

'We'll slide it down,' suggested Fortune. 'I'll take the top, you stand underneath to slow its descent.'

Riddle agreed. 'As soon as the safe started to pick up speed, I realized I had made a misjudgement,' said the burglar from his hospital bed. 'I was no match for it.'

The safe knocked him backwards down the stairs before running over him and breaking both his legs. Arriving at the first landing, it crashed through wooden banisters, then plunged fifteen feet to the floor below. It continued in this way to the basement, making a noise described as a cross between a derailed express and an exploding boiler. The police arrived soon afterwards.

*   *

While attempting to rob the Royal Bank of Scotland at Rothesay, the three raiders became firmly wedged in the revolving door and had to be freed by staff. They retired sheepishly to the street, but returned a few minutes later, on this occasion getting through the door successfully. Unfortunately none of the staff could now take them seriously. When they demanded £50,000 the head cashier simply laughed. Chastened, they lowered their demand to £5,000 but still met broad grins and chuckles. The staff, convinced it was all a practical joke, continued to laugh as the luckless and increasingly desperate robbers came down to £500, then £50 and finally fifty pence. Attempting to leap the counter to snatch money from the till, one of the robbers landed badly, sprained his ankle and was unable to move. The others fled empty-handed only to become stuck yet again in the revolving door.

*   *

An elderly queen coveted a huge tin of caviare in the window of Fortnum and Mason's. Unable to afford the several thousand pounds this delicacy would cost, he hired a professional hoister to steal it for him. This he brilliantly did and £250 changed hands.

On Christmas morning a large party was organized for his friends and cocktails were served. The tin was opened amidst squeals of delight from the assembled company. It proved to be an empty display model.

* *

Entering the Barnsley branch of British Home Stores to do a little hoisting, Mr David Goodall was immediately arrested by eight security men. He had blundered into a store detectives' convention being held in the shop.

DON'T LEAVE TOO MANY CLUES

Asked by his solicitor why he had failed to take the most elementary precautions before carrying out a burglary, John Jessop, aged twenty-three, said he was not so stupid as to do the job without wearing gloves. Unfortunately he had chosen the fingerless variety.

* *

Appearing before the District Court of Baku, Mr Alexei Rachovitz admitted entering a luxury flat and stealing valuables. Impressed by his lavish surroundings he had then taken a bath, shaved and prepared himself a hearty meal while washing and tumble-drying his clothes. After enjoying a bottle of vodka with his meal he began playing the piano and singing so loudly the neighbours complained to the police who called at the flat and arrested him.

*   *

Arrested after being clearly identified on a security camera video recording, bank robber Paul Maclevy, thirty-two, was asked by his solicitor why he had not worn a mask. 'I had a Balaclava over my face when I went into the bank,' he replied, 'but I took it off during the robbery to get a better look at the camera.'

*   *

After their vehicles collided in a Paris street, Albert Rodin and Albert Maurice jumped out, ripped off their dented fenders and began beating each other around the head with them. Police called to the scene arrested both men upon discovering they had stolen the cars.

*   *

Having slipped into the Temperance Hotel and the room of Miss Marian Pascoe and Miss Rhonda Wilder, Mr Arnold G. Robinson, a Minnesota sneak thief, woke the ladies as he rummaged through their luggage for valuables. Leaving their beds they knelt to pray for him, reducing Mr Robinson to tears. He was arrested as he left the room. Temperance Hotel's management had been summoned by a fellow guest who, seeing Robinson enter the bedroom, suspected an orgy was taking place.

*　　*

French forensic experts established the guilt of M. Charles Tubar, wanted for several offences of burglary, by refitting a tooth, which he had accident-ally left in a partially consumed sandwich at the crime scene, into a socket in his gum.

*　　*

Several months after her car had been stolen, Mrs Joan Mail of Greater Manchester was travelling by taxi to a restaurant when she recognized scratches on the rear upholstery. Realizing she was being driven in her stolen vehicle she instructed the driver to take her to the nearest police station and, when they got there, had him arrested.

*　　*

While appearing at the Gaumont, Southampton, a hypnotist billed as the Great Orlando informed his audience he would put twenty of them into a trance.

Approaching the first volunteer, electrician Bob Holliday, he made mystical passes before his face and told him, 'You are deeply asleep.' Mr Holliday remained fully alert but the Great Orlando went out like a light. After waddling around the stage for several minutes doing duck impressions, he confessed to being George Rowson, wanted by the police of four counties for social security frauds.

'I may take up the business professionally,' said Mr Holliday afterwards.

KEEP IN GOOD SHAPE

Arrested for the twentieth time, after driving his getaway car into two parked vans, Philip McCutcheon pleaded guilty to robbery at York Crown Court. Giving him a conditional discharge the Recorder, Mr Rodney Percy, also offered this advice: 'I should give up burglary. In the last few years you have been caught in Otley, Leeds, Harrogate, Norwich, Beverley, York and Hull. You are a man of somewhat distinctive appearance. You have only one eye, an artificial leg, and a withered hand. How can you hope to succeed?'

*   *

Appearing at Knightsbridge Crown Court, Harry Walton admitted an offence of burglary in which, after climbing to the top of a derelict building, he had

fallen through the roof and plunged fifty feet into the basement. When the police arrived Walton scrambled from the rubble, clambered back to the roof and fled across the tiles for half a mile before finally being arrested. Mitigating on his behalf Mr Lawrence Aldrich asked for a lenient sentence on the grounds that although his client had been getting into trouble with the police since 1931, he was now eighty-two years old and suffered from severe arthritis.

*   *

Being stone deaf has proved a serious handicap to Todd Mitchel, fifty-six, a professional burglar. He is constantly being caught by police while still on the premises. 'My problem is I can't hear the alarms go off,' he told his solicitor miserably.

*   *

Despite having his seventeen-year sentence for acting as look-out during an armed robbery confirmed by the Italian Supreme Court, Antonio Pedone has been given a presidential pardon. During the appeal it emerged that Pedone was blind.

*   *

Attempting to rob a Chinese restaurant at Tiverton, Christopher Fleming clambered through a high window, developed vertigo, lost his grip and dropped into the chip fryer. Emerging smothered in cooking oil, he squelched to the till where, finding all the notes had been removed, he filled his pockets with £20 in loose change. His clothes fast congealing, he made an unsteady escape through the front door and into the arms of two policemen.

* *

A 1983 matinée performance of *Snow White and the Seven Dwarfs* at a London theatre was interrupted when officers from Scotland Yard's Robbery Squad raced on to the stage and arrested the dwarf playing Dozey, in connection with a £45,000 bank robbery in Ilford. He had been able to avoid detection up to that point because, being only three-and-a-half feet high, his face had been below the counter and screened from security cameras.

HAVE A MODICUM OF SKILL

A French burglar set the standard for criminal incompetence when, on 4 November 1933, he attempted to rob the home of a Paris antique dealer while dressed in a fifteenth-century suit of armour. After being on the premises a short time he awoke the occupant with his clanking. Going on to the landing, the householder was surprised to see a suit of armour ponderously clambering up the stairs. Waiting until the exhausted burglar had reached the top, he gave him a shove which sent the armoured thief crashing backwards to the ground floor. Following at a more leisurely pace, the antique dealer dropped a small sideboard across his chest to hold him until the police arrived. Unfortunately the weight of the sideboard dented the breastplate making it impossible to free the unfortunate burglar until a blacksmith could be summoned, twenty-four hours later. During this time the burglar was fed through the visor by means of a straw. Asked why he wore the armour he explained, 'To scare him.'

*   *

In his plea of mitigation, Mr Barry Hogan explained that George Gibson could not be described as a sophisticated shop-lifter. 'He first selected a family-size suitcase and then ran through the store from department to department snatching up any goods which took his fancy and throwing them into the case. His has been a life chronicled by misfortune. When he enlisted in the army in 1958 he was sent to the jungles of North Borneo where he was lost for some seven years.

'Returning home he found employment as a gardener but suffered a serious injury while mowing the lawn, when he was struck on the head by a spike thrown from a passing caravan. His first recorded attempt at burglary ended unhappily when, while removing lead from a church roof, he fell on to the altar. He was then charged, in my view improperly, with sacrilege. He tells me that this combination of events led him to start drinking heavily.'

*   *

Keen to steal enough money to impress his girlfriend, David Norris of Croydon wrote a note saying, 'Give me all your cash or I shall shoot!'

'I tried a chemist's shop first, but the girl was too embarrassed to read my message, assuming that it was obscene. Then I went into the sweet shop next door, but the man there said he didn't read English and handed the note back to me. I next tried the Chinese restaurant where the manager claimed that he had lost his glasses and asked me to wait outside whilst he looked for them. Then the police arrived.'

*   *

Appearing for Williams and Shoddy, who had admitted a charge of burglary, Mr John Trot explained, 'My clients had been drinking steadily in the public bar of the Hope and Anchor public house when they ran out of money. Having borrowed a ladder from the landlord, they set it against the building opposite the bar and whilst Williams held the bottom, Shoddy climbed to the first floor where he entered a flat via the bedroom window. Finding a video recorder, he threw it out of the window and hit Williams on the head, stunning him. Recovering, Williams mounted the ladder but shortly afterwards both were on their way to hospital, after taking part in a contest to see who could lean furthest out of the window.'

* *

Pleading guilty to attempted fraud by fiddling his electricity meter, Patrick Maxwell explained that he had turned the ratchet around the wrong way. As a result his next quarter's bill came to £590.

* *

Helmut Wuppertals, an Austrian, forged excellent fifty-mark notes. Except for one small mistake. They were the wrong colour: 'Until my arrest I had no idea I was colour blind,' he explained.

* *

Arrested on counterfeiting charges Olwen Jones, sixty-nine, admitted forging £5 notes using tissue paper, coloured inks and mapping pens. Despite the fact that each note took him more than a month of painstaking labour to produce, the forgeries were so bad that even a partially sighted cashier in a Newport supermarket had no difficulty identifying one as a forgery. 'I did my best. I'm obviously past it,' said Olwen Jones. Asked why he had not forged £10 notes, so doubling his income at a stroke, he replied, 'I never thought of that.'

* *

'When Maurice exhausted the supplies of locally available cheque books and credit cards he set about making his own,' said Mr Alan Banks, prosecuting at Bristol Crown Court. 'Using Letraset he made up cheques for Coutts and Hoares banks. All went well until he ran out of capital Cs, whereupon he changed the name to Toutts. An observant cashier spotted the mistake and called the police.'

* *

When seventy-four-year-old grandmother Ethel West was mugged by a six-foot-tall twenty-year-old while walking through the cloisters of Chichester Cathedral, she grabbed him by the wrist and then put him in an arm lock. 'Oh God, no,' yelled the would-be mugger, 'you're hurting me!'

Freeing himself with difficulty he fled from the scene. 'I'd have put him on his back,' Ethel said afterwards, 'but carrying a full shopping bag slowed me down!'

NEVER MISS A CHANCE

When the wedding reception was in full swing the bridegroom, Mr James McNaulty, was approached by his best man, Mr Paddy Kelly, who explained that an

excellent opportunity for burglary had arisen. Kissing his bride goodbye, and assuring her that he would be only a few minutes, McNaulty drove with Kelly to the home of his bride's mother, Mrs Crackel, and cleared the place out before returning to the reception.

THINK BIG

Charged with stealing 295 tables, 340 typewriters, 959 roll-top desks, 1,069 chairs and 27,056 paper-clips, Professor Mohammed Bikhtami of Isfahan University, Iran, explained it had been a research project. On his release from jail the university appointed him Professor of Criminology.

KEEP YOUR NERVE

Mr Shihaz Patel was serving in his shop in Southall when he was approached by Mr James Dougal, who announced, 'Give me all the money in the till or I will shoot you.'

'I emptied all the money into a bag, and then noticed that Mr Dougal hadn't got a gun at all. I asked him how he intended to shoot me, and he explained that if I didn't hand over the money he would go and get a gun and come back and shoot me then. So I handed it over.'

TAKE PRIDE IN YOUR APPEARANCE

Upset by the Singapore police's description of him as 'warty, low-browed, and scarred', Mr Anthony Hin, wanted for theft, placed an advertisement in the local paper saying he was actually extremely good-looking. Prudently he gave no address.

MAKE SURE OF YOUR GETAWAY

Disturbed by police after breaking into a DIY store, Edward Jones sprinted through eleven demonstration front doors. The last opened on to a brick wall into which he ran full tilt and laid himself out.

*   *

After successfully robbing the Co-op in Perivale, Middlesex, of nearly £5,000, Noel Murray and Andrew O'Conner raced to their getaway car. Attempting to start the engine, O'Conner turned the key the wrong way and jammed the lock. Leaping from the vehicle they scrambled into their second car where O'Conner did exactly the same thing again. At their trial, the prosecution pointed out that, even if either car had been started, it would not have done them much good. The direction they were pointing in would have meant driving straight into the police station.

*   *

Despite the key being left in the ignition, two West Country thieves failed to start a Mini they had stolen from a Truro car park. After attempting to push-start the vehicle for more than two miles, they were stopped by a police patrol and arrested. Only then did the reason for their difficulties become clear. Earlier thieves had stolen the engine.

*   *

Fleeing from a New York bank they had successfully robbed, Ted 'Blood' Splain and Micky 'The Horse' Wilson found their getaway car had vanished. It had been stolen during the few minutes it took to commit the robbery.

*   *

Timothy Watney, of Southend, failed in his attempt to rob the Pleasurerama Amusement Arcade when his getaway car broke down only a few hundred yards from the scene. The car's rear suspension collapsed under the weight of £700-worth of one- and two-penny pieces.

*   *

Armed robber James Lee's big mistake was to ask his girlfriend, Jennifer Nicol, aged twenty, to drive the getaway car for a £13,000 supermarket robbery.

While he held up the store with a sawn-off shot-gun, learner-driver Nicol attempted to park their stolen Ford Sierra near the crime scene. Unfortunately she attracted attention by constantly ramming the cars in front and behind her. This caused the car's false number plates to fall off. Although Nicol coolly fixed them back with elastic bands, suspicions had been aroused and the police were called. Speeding from the scene she crashed into a ditch. Lee is now serving ten years. 'I still love her,' he said.

*   *

Bradley Coventon, a Welsh amateur gunpowder maker, was arrested with two pocketfuls of explosive. While being driven to the police station he jumped from the speeding squad car, landed heavily and exploded.

GET THE PUBLIC ON YOUR SIDE

When he saw a Dobermann pinscher fouling the sidewalk of New York's 11th street, chiropractor Dr Kermit Torick pulled out a pistol and shot it. Arrested and arraigned before a late-night court, Dr Torick explained that although he was a believer in non-violence the sight of 'that huge dog defecating with human-like turds, but larger, much larger, in the middle of the sidewalk,' caused something to snap. 'I've trodden in it all my life. I had to stop it. I got carried away.'

His comments were greeted with cheers by supporters who had packed into the court since his arrest had become known. A woman shouted, 'Dr Torick has done a significant thing. We must all stand by him.'

A pensioner yelled, 'Every time I buy a paper I'm up to my ankles in dog shit. This is a great man. But spitters and litterers are just as bad. They should be shot too.'

'I sympathize with the doctor,' said New York's mayor. 'I also wish the Dobermann a speedy recovery.'

AVOID GOLFERS

Miss Claude Vigil, called to give evidence for the prosecution against Studs Fenelli on a charge of robbery with violence, told the court at Denver, Colorado, 'I was just getting my golf clubs out of the car when Fenelli ran up to me shouting, "Snarl . . . snarl." When I did so, he grasped my jaw and yanked out my false teeth. Then he muttered, "No gold," and threw them into a hedge. As he turned to walk away I caught him behind the left ear with a Number 5 iron, which stunned him until the police arrived.'

TWO

The Boys in Blue

'I have never seen a situation so dismal that a policeman couldn't make it worse.'

Brendan Behan

Your Career in the Police

Don't let the fact that you'll usually be cast in somewhat unsympathetic roles dissuade you from this branch of show business. The costume may not be too appealing – one disgruntled constable complained about the 'baggy, badly cut trousers that won't hold their creases and have flares' – but the pay is excellent and you'll never be without work. Criminals, and even barristers, can experience long periods of 'resting' between parts with nothing to do but sit around and wait for their phone to ring. As a serving officer you'll always get at least a walk-on part.

For speedy advancement from chorus line to star player follow these simple rules:

One – Ensure that you are a member of no minority group except the Masons.

Two – Know your limitations. Modest acting ability – especially when giving evidence – is preferable to occasionally brilliant but uneven playing.

Three – Never upstage a senior officer.

Learning The Language

To get properly into the role and sound convincing you must learn some basic slang. Talking like a proper policeman means using lots of codes designed to impress and confuse your audience. Radioing that you have just observed 'IC3s tooled up and mob handed', for example, sounds much more professional than saying, 'I've seen a gang of armed black men.'

Brief	lawyer
Bent brief	criminal lawyer
Very bent brief	successful criminal lawyer
Club Number	criminal record number
SO1	serious crime
SO6	company fraud
SO8	flying squad
SO10	stolen cars
SO11	criminal surveillance

CRO	Criminal Records Office
DSU	District Support Unit. Exactly the same as the Special Patrol Group (SPG) whose tactics earned such notoriety they had to change the name. Also TSU – Tactical Support Unit.
Form	previous convictions
IC	Identification Code. Also known as RC – Racial Code IC_1 – white caucasian IC_2 – Mediterranean appearance IC_3 – West Indian IC_4 – Asian IC_5 – Chinese (includes Eskimo)
990s	notes taken at an interview. Refers to the printed form.
IRB	Incident report book
Swedey	derogatory term applied by Met detectives to any CID officer working outside London
Wooden Tops	derogatory term used by CID to describe magistrates

MAINTAIN THE AFFECTION OF YOUR AUDIENCE

The Central Ambulance Authority have just issued new headguards to their drivers. 'We had to do something,' explained Chairman Anthony Link. 'They kept on being mistaken for policemen and beaten up!'

*   *

Mr George Stile, promoter of the 'Book a Bobbie for Freedom' campaign, announced that he had now instituted proceedings against some 400 officers for motoring offences at a cost to public funds of several thousand pounds. 'I shall continue to do my duty as a citizen. In any event, I believe my campaign has improved relations between the police and local motorists.' Two of Mr Stiles' recent successes were to report a police officer for failing to protect his tax disc with a transparent waterproof cover and another with unlawfully impeding his rear vision by fixing a rubber 'Pluto' to the back window.

*   *

During a Grand Jury investigation into vice, Memphis housewife Charlotte Tyler, nineteen, said that she had had sex with more than 5,000 police officers, from all ranks, over a three-year period. Explaining her preference for policemen Ms Tyler said, 'I am a strong believer in law and order.'

*   *

Fined for driving without a licence, uninsured and without due care and attention, Mr John Tickle, seventeen, who when stopped had been wearing a World War II gas mask and his sister's see-through housecoat, was asked by magistrates what he intended doing with his life. 'I feel I am cut out for a career in the police,' Tickle replied.

EXPECT ADMIRATION FOR YOUR COSTUME

Arrested for an offence under the Public Order Act, Mr Graham Fido explained that he had been dressed as a gorilla because he was on his way to a fancy dress ball. The arresting officers described how he was swinging from a lamp-post when they first saw him, waving around a cucumber approximately two feet long and describing himself as 'King Dong'.

Refusing to leave his lamp-post, he screamed obscenities at them, drummed his chest, scratched under his armpits and shouted that they had no chance of winning the fancy dress ball themselves, dressed as police officers, a costume which was 'as common as muck'.

*   *

Attending a charity show in aid of police widows at the London Palladium, Sir Robert Mark, then Commissioner of the Metropolitan Police, resplendent in full dress uniform, was taken for the theatre doorman, handed a large number of coats and requested to park several dozen cars.

DON'T RELY ON AUDIENCE PARTICIPATION

To test people's honesty, research psychologist Dr Harold Takooshiam staged some 250 car break-ins which were witnessed by more than 8,000 passers-by. Of these, only twelve made any attempt to stop the offence, some 7,000 pretended not to notice anything, and one man shouted 'I haven't seen a thing' as he raced from the scene. The remainder stopped only to demand a share of the proceeds.

*   *

When a German tourist appeared in Marlborough Street magistrates' court on a shop-lifting charge, proceedings were brought to a halt because none of the officials spoke German and the tourist had no English. 'Is there any member of the public who could interpret?' enquired the magistrate. A punk, complete with ripped leather and full mohican, immediately volunteered. The magistrate explained they must first make sure the right man was in the dock.

'Please ask him his name.'

'No trouble,' replied the punk. Turning to the tourist he screamed, 'UND VOT IST YOUR NAME?'

BE READY TO HELP THE PUBLIC

After taking a statement from a young woman who came to Ndola police station, Zambia, complaining of being threatened by a man with a gun, Constable Phiri told her she was very attractive and asked if he could have sex with her. For this he was prepared to pay ten shillings. She refused at first, but agreed after he raised his offer to fifteen shillings. They made their way to a first-floor lecture hall, where the constable removed all his clothes and requested she did the same.

While they were copulating on the floor, the door opened and the Assistant Commissioner of the Zambian CID entered, accompanied by a group of trainee detectives. The Assistant Commissioner told

Phiri that fornication in the main lecture hall was forbidden. Without pausing the officer replied he was busy taking a statement and they should return in ten minutes.

Phiri later told magistrates, 'I know of no rule preventing love-making in a police station. I undressed out of respect for my uniform.'

*   *

A detective inspector stationed at a West London police station returned from a long, liquid lunch to find a temporary detective constable in the interview room compiling a lengthy list of property stolen during a recent house burglary. Amiably he asked the DC how the interview was getting on.

'Pretty heavy going at the moment, Guv,' was the apologetic reply. 'He seems to have a lot of difficulty remembering all the contents.'

'We'll see about that,' said the DI, grasping a handful of the interviewee's hair with his left hand and punching him in the ear with his right. This was followed by a heavy blow to the chest which sent the man sprawling to the floor. 'That should loosen his tongue a bit,' said the DI. 'Let me know if you have any further problems.'

'He wasn't really being uncooperative,' explained the startled DC. 'He just came in to report the burglary at his own home and was so shaken up he couldn't remember everything that was stolen.'

*   *

George Tywarth, an unemployed cowman, bought an air rifle with the intention of committing suicide. Finding he lacked the courage to kill himself he decided to rob a bank instead. He later told Oxford Crown Court that he had entered the Midland Bank expecting to be caught and sent to prison. When he arrived there was a long queue, so he had to wait. By the time he reached the cashier his courage had failed again so, instead of robbing the bank, he opened an account.

Still determined to be sent to jail, he entered a branch of Barclay's Bank and stole £1,200. When he went to the police station they refused to arrest him, explaining that they were busy dealing with other matters. He was only arrested later that day after accidentally shooting himself in the leg with his air rifle.

*   *

Similar difficulties were experienced by Mr Raymond Bradley, aged twenty-one, of Liverpool when he failed to answer his bail on a charge of unlawfully taking a motor vehicle. Mr Bradley, who had been prevented

from appearing in court due to breaking his leg and collar bone in an accident, obligingly called in at the main Bridewell police station and asked to be arrested. The officers refused because his paperwork had gone missing. A few days later he tried again, with the same result. On the third occasion he was told that although his papers had now been found the officers were too busy to arrest him. The fourth time Mr Bradley was told they were 'full up'. A police spokesman commented, 'At times people stand ten deep to surrender themselves.' 'I just want to be arrested,' complained Mr Bradley. 'It's certainly not for want of trying.'

* *

Giving evidence at his trial for left-wing political agitation in Istanbul, Mr Dursun Karatas claimed that two people had died after being tortured by the security police. Officers guarding the court immediately entered the witness box and beat Mr Karatas unconscious.

* *

M. Alain Vivien, forty-five, and Jean-Pierre Diferro proudly towed a brand-new power boat behind their 504 Peugeot along the Quai États-Unis in Nice. It was a sunny July morning and they were on their way to catch a ferry to Corsica at the start of their holiday.

Suddenly the car ahead braked hard to avoid a child; unable to stop in time Jean-Pierre collided gently with the vehicle in front. Since the car was travelling only ten km per hour, the only damage was two slightly dented fenders. Unfortunately the abrupt stop caused the power boat to slip from its cradle. No serious damage had, at that point, been done to either the cars or the vessel. The owners were congratulating themselves on their good fortune when the police arrived. They closed the street, took everybody's name and ordered a fire brigade mobile crane.

By eleven o'clock this had been manoeuvred into position, ropes and chains attached to the boat, and the process of lifting it back on to the transporter began. When the boat was fifteen feet off the ground its weight proved too much for the strength of the mobile crane which toppled over, dropping the boat on to the Peugeot and crushing a sports car parked nearby. Both vehicles and the vessel suffered serious damage with a bill running into thousands. 'We were just being helpful,' commented a police spokesman.

*   *

Giving evidence in a Spanish court, Chief Superintendent Francisco Javier Fernandez Alvarez explained that 'giving weapons to criminals is a triviality within the routine procedure for catching armed robbers . . .

it is common practice, like that of policemen who have to go to bed with transvestites in order to get information'. He added that on one occasion his men had also supplied guided missiles to terrorists in order to discover how they were supplied with arms.

* *

With the public lavatories of Putney closed and his need urgent, Mr Philip Hercules called in at the local police station and asked to use their toilet. He waited for twenty minutes, sweat streaming down his face, until a sergeant appeared.

'I begged him to allow me to use the toilet,' Mr Hercules told the court, 'but he replied that he was not having me pissing in my shoes in his lavatory. I assured him there was no risk of that since I wanted to do a big job. At that point he ordered me from the station. However, things got out of control. I closed my eyes and just let everything go.' He asked magistrates to increase his sentence from two to three months since this would ensure he had a cell to himself.

* *

A defendant accused the police of assault in the course of arresting him. This was denied by the officer concerned who insisted only reasonable force had been used.

'Perhaps I might demonstrate the hold employed,' the officer suggested. The bench agreed and the usher was asked to serve as a guinea pig. Seizing his arm, the officer brought it up sharply behind his back. A loud crack was heard.

'I seem to have torn his shirt,' the policeman apologized.

The sobbing usher was removed to the hospital where an X-ray showed his elbow had been fractured.

*   *

Hungry and homeless, Henry Connolly was attracted by the light shining under a house door and the sound of merriment from within. Knocking, he asked the man who opened it for the price of a cup of tea. The next thing he knew he was in police custody charged with begging. He had inadvertently banged on the side entrance to Hyde Park police station.

SHOW GREAT INITIATIVE

Sean McGimpsey, wanted by Kildare police for burglary, left his hiding place after Constable Doolan threatened to set his wildly barking police dog on him. When McGimpsey emerged he discovered that PC

Doolan did not actually have a dog, but was merely giving his Alsatian imitation.

'We used to have a police dog,' a police spokesman explained, 'but were obliged to get rid of him as an economy measure.'

* *

Being able to imitate a dog appears to be a valuable police skill. It brought a commendation to PC Judd who, after coming across a flock of sheep which had strayed on to a busy main road, herded them back into the field by crawling on all fours and barking.

* *

For many years the House of Representatives in New Zealand banned the use of police sirens. Instead officers had to lean out of the window and shout warnings of their approach through loud hailers. A police spokesman said, 'Their performance has been remarkably effective, but the practice can be dangerous. This is highlighted by a recent accident involving two officers on a foggy evening.'

* *

Arriving at the scene of an office burglary, Bolton police were surprised to find a German shepherd dog locked inside the building. Releasing it Inspector Alf

Bleasdale had little difficulty in following the animal to the home of its owner, Ernie Fiddler, whom he immediately arrested.

* *

After arresting Mr Abba Owerri, a herbal doctor, Nigerian police strapped him on to the back of a Land Rover and drove him around the town with his genitals displayed. Chief Inspector Aweah explained that the step had been necessary to alert the public to Dr Owerri's quackery. 'He would approach naïve and wealthy citizens offering to shake hands. When they respond Owerri throws himself to the ground shouting that his genitals have disappeared. His bemused victims are then robbed by gangs composed of Owerri's 114 children. This has been going on for years. We hope that by exposing his genitals we shall alert the public to his trickery.'

BE READY FOR UNUSUAL REQUESTS

Arrested by Hollywood police, Frank E. Taylor, aged eighty-six, took advantage of his free call to ask if he could phone Los Angeles international airport with a bomb threat.

* *

Fraud squad detectives who asked to interview Miss Phillida Fagwangle, a victim of Total Allergy Syndrome, about the way in which £65,000 donated to the Save Phillida Fund was spent were told they could do so on certain conditions. Before entering her room they must refrain from the use of tobacco or aftershave for at least two weeks, bath thoroughly and wear night gowns soaked in vinegar.

ANTICIPATE UNUSUAL SITUATIONS

Police executing a search warrant for drugs in Santiago were surprised that one of the guests at a three-day party remained seated in the corner seemingly unperturbed by their presence. This was because he was dead. The host, Snr Miguel Balonez, explained that he was a gatecrasher thought to be called José. He had died the previous evening but rather than spoil the party by making such an announcement it had been decided that he should be left quietly until the following morning.

*   *

During hospital rag week, medical student Tony Tupper removed the penis from a dissection room cadaver and stood on Westminster Bridge with the organ dangling from his flies. A crowd quickly gathered. Tourists took snaps.

When a police sergeant arrived and announced he was arresting Tupper for indecent exposure, the youth snatched the penis from his trousers and flung it into the Thames, shouting, 'There goes your fucking evidence.'

At this point the sergeant and three tourists fainted.

*   *

While keeping watch on Mrs Janakabai Dhangar's unlicensed lemonade factory in Bangalore, plain-clothes officers from the illicit drinking department were attacked by a team of trained monkeys who stripped them naked. The monkeys, three of whom bore the names of famous Indian politicians, had been trained by Mrs Dhangar to protect her premises. The monkeys were outwitted when the detectives returned with supplies of fresh peanuts.

*   *

After a raid on a South Carolina brothel, during which
police arrested 800 customers, the sheriff's office was
inundated with calls from respectable citizens begging

that their names be taken off the charge sheets. The exception was an eighty-three-year-old who offered $100 to be added to it.

HAVE GREAT INTEGRITY

When Sir Robert Mark became Commissioner of Police of the metropolis in the early 1970s, he formed A10, a group of detectives whose job it was to investigate and prosecute corrupt police officers. They decimated the CID and became less than popular with most parts of the force. Information was received by A10 that officers in the Richmond traffic division were lying in wait for motorists outside public houses, breathalysing them and then offering to forget the incident in return for whatever cash the driver had on him. To investigate these allegations, two A10 officers made their way to the pub where they drank a considerable amount and then staggered to their car which they drove erratically for several miles.

Stopped by a traffic patrol the CID driver was breath tested and, when the test proved positive, arrested for driving with excess alcohol. At this point he took £10 from his wallet and asked whether 'something could be done'.

To his surprise he was informed he was being

arrested both for drunken driving and for offering an inducement contrary to the Prevention of Corruption Act.

'I am a detective inspector with A10,' explained the officer, producing his identity card.

'I don't care who you are,' responded the officer. 'You are drunk and you tried to bribe me. You are nicked.'

*   *

PC Michael Waterman, a member of the stolen car squad, was jailed for six months for the theft of a car parked in the police pound. Waterman admitted borrowing the vehicle and driving it to and from work for six months. He was only caught because the car's owner, arrested on a charge of drunkenness, had identified it from his cell window.

*   *

Charged with illegally importing cameras into Thailand, Colonel Chalaw Uthockpatch of Bangkok's Special Branch explained that the equipment had been needed to snap pictures of the ghost of Milly Challibanquer, a Thai star who had fallen to her death from a helicopter some months earlier. The ghost had, he said, appeared to them seated on a sundial in their garden and asked to have its picture taken.

Knowing this would require a first-class camera and electronic flash, Colonel Uthockpatch had smuggled the required items into the country.

'As she has not quite recovered from the multiple injuries occasioned by her fall from the helicopter, the ghost is not as clear as it might be,' he told the enquiry. 'I suggested that she wait to have her picture taken until she was in better health.'

The enquiry, he alleged, was the result of agitation by left-wing atheists who refused to believe his explanation. 'I have photographed President Lincoln and President Roosevelt,' insisted the Colonel. 'It's a well-known fact.'

ENFORCE THE LAW WITHOUT FAVOUR

When meat packer Allen Denny, twenty-three, pinched the bottom of his girlfriend, policewoman Doreen Limpet, during a goodnight embrace she arrested him immediately. 'It was meant to be a compliment,' protested Denny. He was fined £10.

LOOK SMART

Pleading guilty to theft, taking a motor vehicle without consent and attempted burglary, Mr John Kinglegg admitted that he had also impersonated a police officer whose uniform he stole from a patrol car. Mrs Wendy Cricketer became suspicious when Kinglegg called at her home on the pretext of making a phone call: 'I thought it was unusual for an officer of the Metropolitan Police to have a crucifix tattooed on his forehead,' she explained.

BE OBSERVANT

After two years of fruitless searching, police in Davenport, Connecticut, were on the point of closing their files on bank robber Carlo Wilson who had tunnelled his way to freedom from a high-security prison. Then, while watching *The Dating Game* on TV, Police Chief James Prothin recognized Number 1 Bachelor, who claimed to be a debt-collecting agent and part-time clothes designer, as the wanted man. Storming the studio his officers removed the guest at gunpoint. 'He'll have to wait twenty-five years for his next shot at show biz,' says Prothin.

*   *

A Garda spokesman explained that although the body of armed robber James Sweeney, accidentally shot by an accomplice during a bank raid, was laid out for identification by members of the robbery squad who had been watching him for several months, none of them had recognized him.

The spokesman added, 'This is understandable bearing in mind he was still masked.'

*   *

After their kidnapping ordeal Mr Wendover and Mr Swayle Timson recounted their experiences at the hands of the paratroopers who had abducted them.

'Our kidnappers spent much of the evening telling us about their experiences in the Congo where they had taken part in a number of massacres,' said Mr Wendover. 'Leaving us tied hand and foot they went to sleep in the next room. I managed to hop quietly to the telephone and, using my nose, dialled 999. However, the operator refused to connect me unless I would tell her my phone number. This I was unable to do because there was no number on the telephone. Using my mouth to put back the receiver, I dialled directory enquiries. Since I could glimpse a nearby sign through a crack in the window, I was able to provide an address. The operator was helpful but, unable to find the number immediately, offered to call me back with the number. Under the circumstances I felt this would be unwise. I held on and ten minutes later I was able to ring the police.

'When they arrived the paratroopers woke up, untied us and said that we must pretend to be taking part in a business conference. I pointed out that, since we were in a remote, darkened cottage at midnight the explanation seemed improbable. However, I engaged them in conversation about the futures market while trying to drop hints into the conversation with remarks like, "We are a little tied up at the moment." The police eventually demanded our names. Swayle offered to write his down for them, because of the unusual spelling, so he wrote "Help!" on a piece of paper and handed it over. The officer handed it to his inspector who then asked, "And which of you is Mr Help?"'

BLEND WITH YOUR SURROUNDINGS

After spending months disguised as hippies in order to get evidence against a heroin dealer, the drug squad officers had become so involved with the roles that, on bursting into the suspect's house, the detective in charge yelled, 'OK, man. It's the fuzz. This is a bust.'

*   *

Sergeant Richard DeClara, one of New York's finest, patrolled Grand Central Station wearing only his boots, socks, police cap and holster. Exchanging pleasantries with passengers, he asked a black man, 'When did you find yourself turning black? Did you find yourself eating watermelon, tap dancing and shining shoes?'

His unconventional policing methods attracted the attention of CBS who secretly filmed him for the six o'clock news. 'This is just revenge for the public suspension of our chief, John Esposito, who was indicted for criminal misuse of a police computer,' said one of his fellow officers. 'His actions are a humiliation to us all,' complained Mario Cuomo, the Governor of New York. A union spokesman dismissed DeClara's nude patrol as 'harmless horseplay'.

*   *

During the thirties, Detective Inspector George Eustace of Brixton CID gained a considerable reputation for his mastery of disguise. On one occasion he jumped on to a marble pedestal and posed as a religious statue in order to observe the actions of a thief inside a nunnery.

'I did not blink an eye even when a fly landed on my nose,' commented Inspector Eustace. 'When imitating statues remaining motionless is of the utmost importance.'

'His make-up as a Jewish receiver of stolen property

has long been the admiration of the detective service,'
said a colleague.

*   *

As toddlers queued to sit on Santa's lap in California's
Monterey Park Shopping Center, a mother and child
pushed to the head of the line and demanded drugs.

'The stuff's in my toy bag,' responded Santa
smartly. 'That will be $30.'

Revealing herself as an undercover narcotics agent,
the woman immediately arrested Santa, leading him
away in handcuffs to the wails of disappointed
children.

BE PATIENT WITH MOTORISTS

PC Borough explained to the court that to make for
more harmonious police–public relations, he would
sometimes make use of an intermediary in the
decision to prosecute.

'When I stop motorists in spot checks and discover
defects in their vehicles, I place my Sooty glove puppet
over my right hand and say to the driver, "This is a
difficult one, how about we let Sooty decide?" Then
Sooty whispers in my ear, I turn to the motorist and

say, "Sooty says you are booked, Sir, so I'm afraid that's that."'

*   *

Mr Peter Clapper, of Bodmin, was arrested on suspicion of driving while unfit after officers saw him trying to enter his car via the tail-gate while it was wedged between two bollards.

An examination of his driving documents revealed that his licence was unsigned. Asked to comply with this requirement he wrestled, unsuccessfully, with the plastic cover for five minutes. After finally managing to uncap his fountain pen he signed his name on the arresting officer's forehead.

*   *

Giving evidence at Eastbourne magistrates' court a police sergeant explained that he had followed Mr Harper, aged eighty-seven, over a distance of 700 yards during which time his speed never exceeded thirteen mph.

'On stopping the vehicle, I asked Mr Harper to get out and, in view of his age and apparent infirmity, take an eye-sight test. Pointing to a vehicle about ten yards away I asked him to read off the number plate. Whereupon he replied, "What vehicle?"

'As he claimed not to remember his own number plate, I suggested he try reading that since it was somewhat closer. He then got down on his hands and knees, crawled up to the number plate and still misread it from a distance of six inches. His passenger, Mrs Joan Lagher, informed me Mr Harper was registered blind but would say no more as it was dangerous to talk to the police.'

*   *

Called to a serious traffic accident, Redditch police officers found Mr Rough's Rover embedded in the body of Mrs Rough's two-tone Toyota. Interviewed in her hospital bed, Mrs Rough explained the last thing she could remember was going to collect their children. Mr Rough recalled arriving home early from a business appointment. The crash had occurred in the semi-circular driveway of their home.

*   *

'I could hear the car from at least a mile away,' Garda O'Connor told a Dublin court. 'It sounded like a bomb going off. When I approached the vehicle it was travelling about five mph. After ordering the driver to stop I examined the vehicle and found that it only had first gear, no brakes at all, a flat battery, poor steering, a flat spare tyre, no hub caps or driving mirrors, and was covered in mud. As I was looking at the car the exhaust dropped off and the engine boiled over. The driver, Mr Rooney, was very co-operative.'

Mr Rooney explained he had paid a passer-by £6 for the vehicle as he needed transport to get himself to hospital after breaking a leg when his own car fell on him as he was jacking it up to change a flat tyre. 'My broken leg was the only reason I was driving un-insured,' he said, and added that he and his wife hoped to sell their new vehicle to a motor museum.

*   *

While parked in a Gloucester safari park, Mr and Mrs John Swaine of Truro, Cornwall, had their car sat on by an elephant. An apologetic management offered them a free lunch, with two bottles of wine, by way of compensation. This they accepted. Driving home the couple were stopped by a police patrol who wanted to know why the rear of their vehicle was crushed.

When Mr Swaine explained the damage had been caused by an elephant he was immediately breathalysed, found to be over the limit and arrested. He was subsequently fined £60 and banned from driving for a year.

YOU MUST PUT UP WITH ENDLESS FRUSTRATIONS

A van containing sophisticated electronic surveillance equipment and secret documents was stolen recently in Belfast. A Special Branch spokesman explained that attempts to find the truck had been impeded by the fact that issuing any description of it would be a breach of the Official Secrets Act.

*　　　　*

Mr Datuk Hassan Ibrahim, the Indian Minister of Pensions, says his office has been defrauded by millions of dollars each year by thieves using thumbs amputated from dead pensioners. These are used to continue drawing a person's benefits after they have died by marking their book with the relevant print. One pensioner, who had apparently been drawing his allowance since 1862, was mentioned in the *Calcutta Herald* as the oldest man in the world. His address turned out to be a cinema. A police investigation came to nothing when, in the space of three days, 567 of the claimants died in a mysterious epidemic.

*　　　　*

A submission of no case to answer was upheld on behalf of Mr Donald McAulay after an X-ray photograph, produced to establish that he had swallowed the ignition key of a van he was trying to steal, was excluded on the grounds that police had obtained it without a search warrant.

*　　　　*

The Court of Appeal in Colorado has determined that to laugh at a person in custody is not *per se* a ploy to assist in obtaining a confession. The court was considering the case of one Jedd Sloeman who was arrested outside the warehouse of the Globe Freezer Company in possession of a large plastic sack. When approached by Special Investigator Drury and asked what was in the sack, he claimed not to know. Opening it Drury discovered 1,800 frozen animal rectums. 'I chuckled as I told him the news that he had stolen a bag of arseholes,' said Drury. 'Sloeman then confessed to the burglary, begging me to book him on a manslaughter charge as, otherwise, he would be the victim of endless cruel jokes in prison.'

*   *

San Francisco teenager Davin Fuller, who stole a city bus for a joy ride, was awarded $150,000 damages by a jury for having his civil rights violated by the police officer who arrested him.

YOU'LL BE EXPOSED TO MORE THAN NORMAL TEMPTATION

When Joseph Ferreris and his partner Mimi Setters were arrested on a charge of indecency arising from their Dance of Love at the Bottoms Up nightclub,

Judge Irving Shaw went with the jury to observe their act. It involved copulation on a bearskin rug. Unable to decide whether intercourse had actually occurred, the judge requested an encore. Since the defendants were in no state to oblige, the act was repeated by understudies. Sympathizing with the judge's dilemma, NYPD detective George Ulrich revealed that his officers had seen the show seventy-five times. Asked by a lady juror whether he had become sexually aroused, Ulrich explained, 'Police officers are not responsive to normal stimuli.'

* *

After waiting on Florida's death row for eleven years, two black men are to be re-tried with defence lawyers confident of an acquittal. Their optimism arises from the fact that, much to police annoyance, the defendant can no longer remember whether she was raped or not.

YOU WILL BE WORKING WITH HIGHLY TRAINED PROFESSIONALS

Dr Mario Fuselli, a consultant psychologist engaged by the Lima police to interview a man suspected of several murders, called a press conference to explain the result of his interrogations. 'I spent several days with Balbino in the course of which he confessed to a series of hideous crimes. I was so disgusted that I decided that in the interests of humanity I must put an end to his career of violence. So I strangled him with my belt.'

*   *

The Tokyo police have formed a special riot squad composed of disabled ex-servicemen, many with only one eye and some with artificial limbs. The squad, to be known as Tingo-Ta, has been formed to deal with demonstrations by women, pensioners and other 'naturally handicapped persons'.

*   *

Sergeant Bob Haslett explained that he had been on duty at Launstone police station when he received an emergency call. 'I suspected the caller had been the victim of a serious attack as he appeared incapable of speech. I could hear only heavy breathing and a sort of choking, rasping noise. Assuring him that help was on its way, I offered consolation and encouragement for the next thirty minutes until officers arrived at the address which had been traced through the operator. Effecting a forcible entry they discovered Domingo, a golden retriever, alone in the house with a push-button phone whose handset he had been nibbling and licking whilst I spoke to him.'

*   *

Having received a call that a safe had been abandoned on the verge of a road near Halesowen, West Midlands police ordered it dusted for fingerprints by a Scenes of Crimes officer and sent a tow truck to remove it. Only then did they discover it was an electricity board junction box concreted into the ground.

*   *

Officers at Spiddal Garda station were embarrassed when, during an official inspection, a skeleton with a bullet hole in the left temple tumbled out of a cupboard at the superintendent's feet. In an attempt to solve the mystery, Garda Duffy – the station's longest-serving officer – was asked what he knew of it. Duffy said he believed it had been washed ashore during the French Revolution but could not say for certain on which beach. He explained he had suffered from severe memory loss since he slipped on a discarded tuna fish sandwich during a Garda ball and landed on his head.

*   *

Seeing Mr William George apparently asleep in his car in Beacon Street, Boston, and receiving no response to a tap on the window, traffic warden Gerry Sachs issued a ticket. Two hours later, finding the car and driver in the same place, he gave him another ticket. He continued doing so for six hours until there was no space remaining on the windscreen. On opening the door to remonstrate with Mr George he found him dead from a bullet wound to the neck.

SHOULD YOU FAIL TO MAKE IT INTO THE REGULAR POLICE, PRIVATE DETECTION CAN PROVE REWARDING

'I really wanted to become a police officer,' explained Mrs Dora Beadwell on her retirement after twenty-three years as a store detective, 'but my height was against me. I am only four foot six tall. However, since this was the dawn of the supermarket era, I decided to become a store detective. My most important skill has been to be in the right place at the right time. I once concealed myself for five days in a giant carrier bag in order to apprehend a persistent thief.

'I count among my major successes occasions when I have arrested a bishop's wife leaving the store with a hamster concealed in her hat, and a senior police officer whom I caught with five fillet steaks down his trousers. I have, in my career, arrested headmasters, nuns, matrons, vicars and war heroes. My worst moment was when I caught my next door neighbour. It was so embarrassing I was obliged to move house.

'One of my most dangerous assignments was to secrete myself on top of a ceiling heater from which I observed the general manageress having carnal knowledge of a dustman. This secured her dismissal but they escaped prosecution as there was no pecuniary loss.'

OR YOU CAN JUST PRETEND TO BE A POLICEMAN

Following his arrest, Mr Samar Loang of Sendai, Japan, admitted impersonating a police officer for some twenty-four years. He explained that his luxury home with its swimming pool had been entirely financed by on the spot fines extracted from speeding motorists. Asked why it had been necessary to promote himself to Chief District Superintendent, Mr Loang said he had no choice. Without a more senior rank he could not explain away his remarkable prosperity.

THREE

Careers in Court

'No brilliance is needed in the law. Nothing but
common sense, and relatively clean fingernails.'

John Mortimer, A Voyage Round My Father

The multi-millionaire American banker, John Pier-
pont Morgan, once remarked, 'I don't want a lawyer
to tell me what I cannot do. I hire him to tell me how
to do what I want to do.'

It's a distinction you should keep firmly in mind if
you decide to enter this highly lucrative branch of
judicial show business. The lawyers' role is never to
distinguish truth from falsehood but to act out, with
all the histrionic power at their command, a part
largely written by their clients. As the poet Robert
Frost pointed out, 'A jury consists of twelve persons
chosen to decide who has the better lawyer.' He might
just as fairly have said the 'better performer'.

Solicitors

Although they can act as minor stars in the repertory theatres of the law, also known as magistrates' courts, their main business is acting as agents for the superstars of jurisprudence, the barristers.

However, just as theatrical agents usually do far better out of show biz than most of their clients, solicitors can make up in hard cash what they lack in glamour. Join their ranks and you'll be entering a boom business. In 1965 there were 20,000 solicitors in private practice in England and Wales, today there are nearly 50,000 and the number is rising all the time. The current legal aid budget for criminal work is £62 million. A well-established London solicitor specializing in crime could expect to gross around £100,000 per annum.

Barristers

They are the superstars of the law. To ensure success you should be white, middle class, and male – only thirteen per cent of barristers are women – and have a public school education. At first you'll be playing to unsympathetic audiences on provincial stages far from the glitz of the Old Bailey. You'll start by making hopeless bail applications and unbelievable pleas in mitigation before bored stipendiaries and hostile lay magistrates.

Criminal work is the least well paid, so if your main interest in the law is making large amounts of money stick to the commercial stage where half of all barristers practise.

Earnings here range from £80,000 net to over £1 million a year. On the criminal side, things are less financially rosy, but average earnings still top £30,000 a year. But since it can take a newly qualified barrister many years to enjoy this level of income some private money is advisable.

Judges

They are best compared to theatre critics. Like them they observe the drama with a cynical eye, sum up the performers and then tell the audience – in their case the jury – what they ought to make of the show.

Becoming a judge is a form of early retirement for barristers, with the added advantage of a substantial pension. As a High Court judge you can expect to earn £65,000 a year together with such perks as a luxurious home while on tour, a chauffeur-driven car, member-

ship of the most exclusive clubs and the possibility of a
seat in the Lords to crown your show biz career.

Lay Magistrates

They are the amateur players. There is no need to
audition for a part. If you pass a secret audition
conducted by a neighbourhood committee your name
will automatically be put forward to the Lord Chancellor for consideration. Since these committees meet
behind closed doors it's difficult to know precisely
what qualities are needed to join the 21,000-strong
cast.

As in all other branches of the law, a sound working
knowledge of the professional lingo is essential for
success. Here are the lines most commonly heard in
court.

What Is Said	*What Is Meant*
'If you please . . .'	'Like it or lump it.'
'If your Lordship pleases . . .'	'Oh, if you must.'
'I am much obliged . . .'	'Thanks for nothing.'
'I am very greatly obliged . . .'	'I'm hoping for a seat on the bench.'

'With respect . . .'

'I am about to be extremely rude.'

'Be that as it may . . .'

'What's that got to do with anything, you dickhead?'

'I suggest you are mistaken . . .'

'I suggest you are lying through your teeth.'

This expression is used to avoid directly accusing a witness of lying, since if you do so your client's deplorable criminal record may be revealed.

'In my submission . . .'

'What I think happened.'

'My learned friend . . .'

'My half-witted opponent.'

'Would now be a convenient moment . . .?'

This is used by barristers whenever they are dying for a drink/a pee/to go home and watch the test match and so on. The traditional response is for the judge immediately to order an adjournment.

'On account of costs.'

'Give me some money.'

'On account of disbursement.'

'I want more money.'

'Put in funds.'   'I want even more
                                  money.'

'A retainer.'   'I want lots of money.'

'A brief fee.'   'A huge sum of money.'

To enjoy a long and prosperous career keep the
following points in mind.

YOU MUST BE DEDICATED

Certain he would fail the California state bar exams
for the second time, Mr Morgan Lamb persuaded his
lawyer wife to dress in man's clothes and impersonate
him. This she did, achieving the third highest marks
out of 7,000 candidates. Their deception was discovered, not because Morgan Lamb had previously
failed so dismally, but because his wife was seven
months pregnant. 'This is a case of yuppie greed run
amok,' said the prosecutor.

*   *

Having passed his Law Society examinations at the
twenty-sixth attempt, Mr John Crisp died, aged 102,
the day before he was due to receive his practising
certificate. Deciding to award it posthumously, an
official explained, 'His dearest wish was to practise at

the Bar, and his death should not be allowed to come in the way of that ambition.'

HAVE A STRONG SENSE OF YOUR OWN SUPERIORITY

On one occasion the barrister F. E. Smith, later Lord Birkenhead, had made a lengthy and articulate presentation of complex legal arguments. After listening intently the judge remarked sourly, 'I regret I am none the wiser.'

'No wiser, my Lord, I accept,' responded F. E. Smith, 'but infinitely better informed.'

*   *

Representing his client at a provincial magistrates' court, a London barrister became increasingly irritated by frequent interventions from the clerk of the court. Finally he snapped at the chairman of the bench: 'Really, Sir, when one is addressing the organ grinder, it is intolerable to be interrupted by his monkey.'

CULTIVATE SOME AMIABLE ECCENTRICITIES

Barrister Billy Reece-Davis, known affectionately as the One-Armed Bandit, has a formidable reputation for attacking prosecution witnesses with a vigour that sometimes causes less flamboyant colleagues to quail.

On one occasion, while he was attacking a police witness, his learned junior became so concerned he tried to attract the Bandit's attention by plucking at his robes. When this brought no response he hastily scribbled a note of caution and passed it to his leader. This too Billy Reece-Davis ignored.

'You have been passed a note,' the judge observed.

'Oh, just a billet-doux, I imagine, my Lord,' Billy replied.

'More, I suspect, a Billy don't,' retorted the judge.

*   *

An idiosyncratic member of the Bar returned from an excellent lunch to make his closing speech to the jury in defence of a burglar at Snaresbrook Crown Court. Unusually, he lit a cigar before rising to his feet and, using it to emphasize his remarks, said, 'Members of the jury, now is the time for my learned friend who prosecutes to restate the facts of the prosecution case, for me to urge upon you the arguments in favour of the defendant, for the learned judge to restore the balance by summing up both sides of the argument, and for you to bring in a true verdict according to the evidence. The difficulty is the prosecutor is too dull to make a speech of any kind, I am too pissed to remember the defence, the judge is far too biased to sum up fairly, and by the looks of things you lot are too stupid to bring in any sort of verdict.'

On another occasion, making his closing remarks before a rather deaf judge, he said very softly, 'Members of the jury, the time has come for me to take off all my clothes. Indeed, we should all take off our clothes, you, the prosecutor, every one of us. For I want you to come and bathe with me in a pool of common sense.'

Fiddling urgently with his deaf aid and seriously alarmed at what little he had managed to hear, the judge attempted to interrupt. 'And of course your Honour must come along as well,' said the barrister reassuringly, 'as the bath attendant.'

Essential Acting Skills

THE ABILITY TO KEEP A STRAIGHT FACE

Appearing at Undercliffe magistrates' court, Hastings, Mr Geoffrey Jones contested the charge of criminal damage brought after he had allegedly used a hatchet to demolish the partition wall between him and his neighbour who did his washing at four o'clock every morning. Mr James Willow, for the defendant, explained his client had been awakened by the sound of rushing water and, as he leaped from the bed, his pyjama trousers had dropped to his ankles causing him to fall heavily against the wall which gave way beneath his weight. When the police arrived he had been holding the hatchet – purely with a view to repairing the wall as quickly as possible.

*   *

In his plea of mitigation, Mr Simon Johnson explained that the defendant, Peter Burr of Fife, had seen a lorry carrying whisky jack-knife and spill part of its cargo on the road ahead of him. He had taken off his trousers in order to mop up the spilled spirit and stood by his car wringing them out into the windscreen washer bottle. He was sucking and chewing on them when the police arrived and arrested him for indecent exposure.

*   *

Asked by the judge to explain his failure to return to court following an adjournment, Mr James Cross, who was charged with attempting to steal a car, explained he had been delayed because he was trying out the technique demonstrated by the prosecuting counsel the previous day.

*   *

Mitigating on behalf of a client charged with the cultivation of more than 300 cannabis plants Mr Jones told Penrith Crown Court that he was instructed to explain that his client had been going to buy a parrot but, before doing so, thought that he should secure a supply of seeding plants so that the parrot would not be a burden to the household budget. He had bought what he believed to be sunflower seeds. These had proved to be cannabis. His interest then switched to horticulture and he had decided to cultivate the plants, although still without realizing they were cannabis, as a main crop.

When the judge interrupted to ask why, shortly before his arrest, he had been seen uprooting the plants and throwing them over the hedge into his neighbour's garden, Mr Jones explained, 'My client had by then lost interest in both birds and plants, and decided to buy a dog instead.'

*   *

Giorgio Spiler was acquitted of outraging public decency following his arrest while dancing, in the Piazza San Marco, dressed as a giant penis. The judge found no case to answer after Spiler's lawyer, Carlo Prossi, pointed out that during celebrations the previous year his client had danced while disguised as a monster vagina without being arrested.

A VIVID IMAGINATION

Speaking in mitigation on behalf of Mr Donald Reece, who, as a postman, had stolen giros to the value of over £18,000, Mr Mark Donaldson said the cause of his client's financial difficulties really lay with the police.

They had identified a corpse washed up near Beachy Head, Eastbourne, as his elder brother Harry. As his closest relative Reece had been responsible for the funeral costs which had been very considerable. Only two days after the funeral, he had received a letter from Harry who was alive and well and on holiday in Bournemouth. A fortnight after that the Dorset police had contacted him with the news that Harry had died playing miniature golf. This time the information was correct but had led to a second funeral followed by a further costly wake. Donald had been impoverished and Harry had left him nothing in his will.

*   *

Defending a driver charged with travelling down London's Edgware Road at more than ninety mph, his lawyer admitted his client's guilt but explained, 'He believed he was being sucked into the middle of a Black Hole.'

YOU SHOULD BE QUICK-WITTED

When the barrister defending a motorist charged with motorway speeding asked how the officer could be sure of his client's speed, the policeman replied that he had been on motorway patrol for years and could tell how fast a car was travelling at a glance.

Flinging his pencil into the air with a dramatic gesture, counsel demanded, 'And how fast was that travelling?'

Without a moment's hesitation the policeman replied, 'Forty-two miles per hour.'

*   *

Mr Peter Ellis appeared at Knightsbridge Crown Court to prosecute a skinhead charged under two sections of the Offences Against the Person Act with a serious assault on an elderly man. He had been identified by the complainant, but there was virtually no other evidence against him. The skinhead was represented by a learned counsel, the author of several books warning law students against those errors to which young advocates are prone.

After conferring with his client, he approached Mr Ellis to find out whether there was any possibility of the prosecution accepting a plea to a very much less serious offence. Mr Ellis said he doubted it, but would have a word with the officer concerned.

On doing so he discovered that the unfortunate complainant had died from natural causes some weeks earlier. Returning to defence counsel he said he had managed to persuade a reluctant officer to drop the charge of grievous bodily harm and accept the less serious offence of actual bodily harm in return for a guilty plea. The defending barrister was duly grateful.

Opening the case to the judge, Peter Ellis was able to enjoy even greater satisfaction from the arrangement when he told the court, 'Your Honour will no doubt give this young man the usual credit for his guilty plea and the contrition that he thereby expresses. The more so in this case because owing to the unfortunate death of the complainant, had he not, in accordance with his counsel's advice, pleaded guilty, I would have been quite unable to proceed against him on either of these charges.'

*   *

Cross-examining the first mate of a trawler which had collided with a Royal Navy destroyer, a barrister asked, 'What did the skipper say when the destroyer appeared off your port bow?'

'He said, "Bugger me."'

'He said what?' demanded the judge.

'The witness is suggesting he was somewhat taken aback,' the barrister explained.

*   *

Defence Attorney Clark Head of Sonora, California used farting as the basis of an appeal against his client's conviction on a charge of breaking and entering.

He complained that Tuolumne County Assistant District Attorney Ned Lowenbach 'farted about 100 times' during his closing speech to the jury.

'He just kept doing it, as if to show disrespect for me, my case and my client,' Clark Head explained. 'He continually moved around and ripped pieces of paper throughout the trial. And then he would fart again. It was impossible to concentrate . . . The closing speech is supposed to be sacred. It's like the defendant's last chance and you aren't supposed to interrupt it. Certainly not by farting.'

HAVE A SENSE OF HUMOUR

During a civil suit for damages against the Coal Board, the judge became increasingly irritated by the pedantic manner in which a miner was giving evidence. Finally he demanded of the man's counsel, 'Is your client familiar with the doctrine of *res ipsa loquitor* [the facts speak for themselves]?'

'My Lord,' replied the barrister, 'I understand that in Huddersfield they speak of very little else.'

* *

At the conclusion of an armed robbery trial at St Albans Crown Court, the members of the Bar involved decided to hold a dinner in honour of the judge. Accordingly they booked several rooms in a local hotel.

The senior counsel, a dedicated prosecutor and Establishment man with his eye firmly fixed on a seat on the bench, went to have a bath leaving one of his more exuberant colleagues, Mr Patrick Packingham, alone in the bedroom. At that moment a telephone call came through from the Lord Chancellor's Department inviting the senior counsel to sit as an Assistant Recorder the following week.

Packingham, who took the call, exclaimed in a high-pitched, effeminate voice that the gentleman concerned was taking a bath but that he would happily take any message since he was his boyfriend.

The horrified counsel had heard enough of the conversation to leap from the bath and run naked into the room. By then Packingham had hung up, leaving the wretched man with the unenviable choice of either attempting an explanation or seeing his hopes of judicial advancement shattered.

MAINTAIN AN ABILITY TO KEEP COOL UNDER TRYING CIRCUMSTANCES

Apologizing to an Old Bailey court for not wearing his wig, barrister Colin Hart-Leverton explained, 'It was blown off my head in the course of a bomb explosion and carried off by a tourist as a souvenir.'

CHOOSE YOUR CAST OF SUPPORTING PLAYERS WITH CARE

Called as a character witness for her friend, Mrs Beatrice Press made a somewhat unsteady appearance in court. After collapsing on her way to the witness box she had to be carried out by court officials. On returning and being asked by his Honour Judge Shawfield whether she had been drinking, Mrs Press admitted consuming four cans of extra-strong lager, half a bottle of whisky and four quarts of beer before attempting to enter the witness box. The learned judge reminded Mrs Press that, some two weeks earlier, she had appeared before him to give character evidence on behalf of her husband. On that occasion she claimed to be a strict teetotaller who never allowed drink into the house. The ideal person, in fact, to reform an alcoholic.

*   *

The following exchange took place at Stratford magistrates' court.

CLERK: Say, 'I swear by Almighty God.'

MR PERRY (*a witness*): Yes.

CLERK: Repeat after me, 'I swear by Almighty God –'

MR PERRY: I swear by Almighty God . . .

CLERK: 'That the evidence I give –'

MR PERRY: That's right.

CLERK: Repeat it.

MR PERRY: Repeat it.

CLERK: No, repeat what I said.

MR PERRY: I can't remember what you said.

CLERK: What I said when?

MR PERRY: I can't remember.

CLERK: Yes – 'That the evidence I give –'

MR PERRY: Yes – that the evidence I give.

CLERK: No, not yes. Just 'that the evidence I give'.

MR PERRY: What, 'just that the evidence I give'?

CLERK: 'Shall be the truth –'

MR PERRY: It will, and nothing but the truth.

CLERK: Repeat what I say . . .

MR PERRY: I am no scholar, you know.

CLERK: We can appreciate that. Just say, 'Shall be the truth and . . .'

MR PERRY: Shall be the truth and –

CLERK: Say 'nothing'.

MR PERRY: 'All right' (*remains silent*).

CLERK: No, don't say nothing, say 'nothing but the truth'.

MR PERRY: Yes.

CLERK: Can't you say 'nothing but the truth'?

MR PERRY: Yes.

CLERK: Well, do so.

MR PERRY: You are confusing me.

CLERK: Just say 'nothing but the truth'.

MR PERRY: Is that all?

CLERK: Yes.

MR PERRY: All right, I understand.

CLERK: Then say it.

MR PERRY: What?

CLERK: 'Nothing but the truth.'

MR PERRY: But I do. That's it.

CLERK: You must say 'nothing but the truth'.

MR PERRY: I will say nothing but the truth.

CLERK: Please just repeat the words 'nothing but the truth'.

MR PERRY: What, now?

CLERK: Yes, now. Yes . . . just say those words.

MR PERRY: Nothing but the truth.

CLERK: Thank you.

MR PERRY: I'm just not a scholar.

*   *

To demonstrate the weakness of eye-witness evidence against his client, Attorney Nigel Armstrong invited nineteen-year-old Robert Holt, whom he found in the corridor of a Florida court, to sit in the defendant's chair while his client sat among the spectators. He then watched with satisfaction as three different witnesses identified Mr Holt as his client. But when he revealed his ruse to the court, Judge Warren Conklin told him he believed the witnesses. A protesting Mr Holt was jailed for twelve months.

NEVER ASK A QUESTION UNLESS CERTAIN OF THE ANSWER

The chief witness against a motorist charged with dangerous driving was a middle-aged woman cyclist who had been overtaken by the accused immediately before the accident. An excellent witness who gave her evidence clearly and confidently, she made a favourable impression on judge and jury.

There was, she insisted, absolutely no doubt in her mind that the car had been travelling at more than eighty miles an hour when it passed her.

'You are certain on that point,' insisted the prosecuting counsel.

'There is no shred of doubt in my mind at all,' she replied firmly.

He then asked one further, fatal, question. 'And how fast do you estimate you were cycling?'

'Approximately sixty miles an hour.'

*   *

A West Country farm-hand was charged with having intercourse with a duck. The chief witness was a cowman who had passed the duck pond on his way to the milking shed and seen the incident. Prosecuting counsel was taking him through the events of that morning. The exchange, aided by a detailed plan of the farmyard, went as follows:

'On the morning of July 25th did you go from the farmhouse, which is marked A on the chart, down the footpath, B, to the cowsheds, indicated by the letter C?'

'Yes, sir.'

'And as a result you went within a few yards of the duck pond which is indicated by the letter D?'

'I did, sir.'

'And did you observe anything.'

'I did, sir.'

'Will you tell his Lordship and the jury what you saw.'

'I saw George Smith.'

'You saw the accused?'

'Yes.'

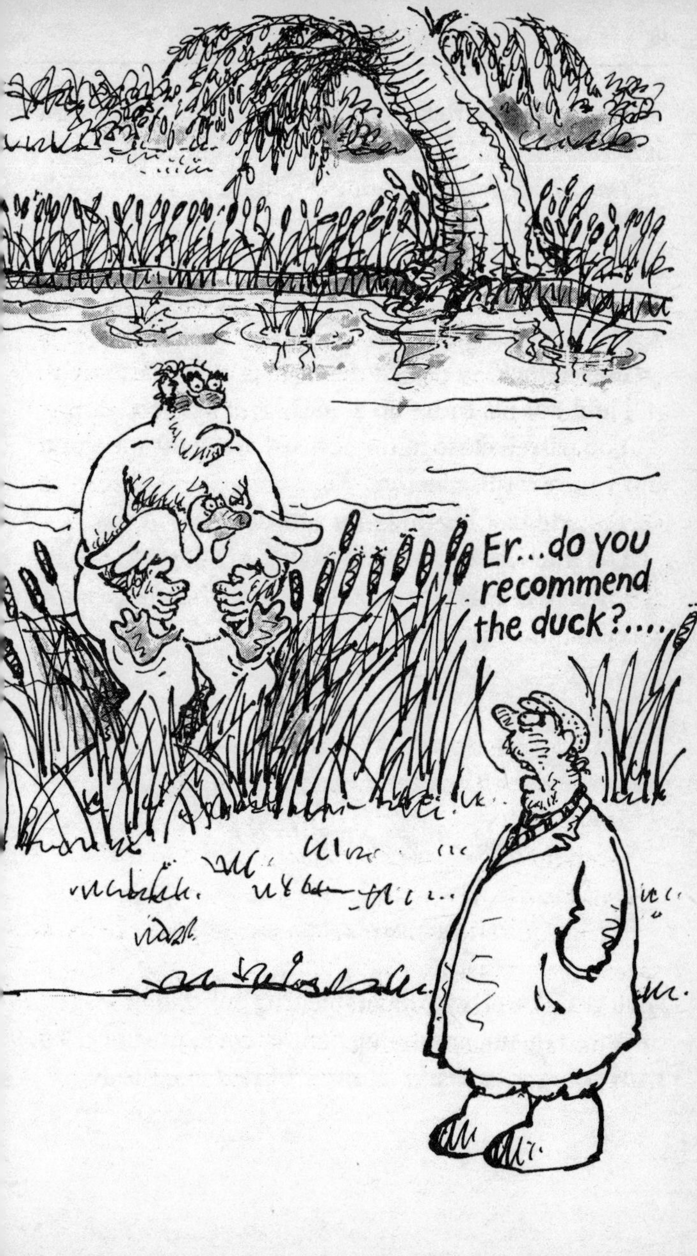
Er...do you recommend the duck?.....

'Can you tell the court what George Smith was doing?'

'Yes.'

'Well, will you kindly do so.'

'He was putting his thing into a duck.'

'His thing?'

'His penis.'

'Into a duck?'

'He'd got his thing up a duck.'

'You passed close to the accused, the light was good and you saw this clearly?'

'Yes. He had his thing up a duck.'

'Did you say anything to him?'

'Of course I did.'

'What did you say?'

'Mornin', George.'

Magistrates Need to Be . . .

IMPARTIAL

'You're an utterly disreputable trio,' a London magistrate told the men standing before him in the dock, 'so I am going to remand all three of you in custody.'

'Only the one in the middle,' protested the officers accompanying the prisoner.

*   *

'There's certainly an element of doubt in this case,' agreed a Highbury magistrate on hearing the defence submissions. Then glowering at the defendant he added, 'But don't think you're going to get the benefit of it!'

ALERT

During a particularly unpleasant rape case, the young female victim found herself overcome with embarrassment when asked to provide details of the assault. The chairman agreed she could write down the lurid details. This she did and the note was passed to the chairman who read it with disgust. The note was handed to a lady magistrate on his right who expressed even greater revulsion. Finally it was handed to the third magistrate, an elderly man who had been dozing quietly during much of the trial.

Jerked back to full consciousness as the note was thrust into his hand he read it quickly, stared at the witness in astonishment then, nodding delightedly, thrust the note into his pocket.

TOLERANT

The Brighton Licensing Justice granted a two-hour extension for the bars of the Municipal Conference Centre on the occasion of the annual weekend conference of Alcoholics Anonymous.

PREPARED TO OFFER THE BENEFIT OF THE DOUBT

'I was not standing naked at the window, but merely passing between bedroom and bathroom in a state of normal undress,' explained Mr Harry Boggle during his trial for indecent exposure. Asked why, moments earlier, he had been peeping over the window ledge, Mr Boggle told the court, 'I was looking for a mouse in the back garden which I intended to shoot.'

'The strangeness of his story contains a ring of veracity,' commented the magistrate.

DEFENDERS OF THE INNOCENT

Donald Capper and John Wilkinson appeared at Clerkenwell magistrates' court charged with a breach of the peace. Police explained that the men, both dressed as Santa Claus, had been fighting over a lucrative pitch. During their struggle beards had been pulled off, red robes torn and hats stomped into the snow.

Passing sentence, the magistrate remarked sternly, 'Seeing two Santas engaged in such a violent altercation could shatter a young child's belief in the magic of Christmas.'

* *

Metropolitan stipendiary magistrate the late Mr Lowdon, was notorious among lawyers for his ferocity and habit of drinking two bottles of sweet white wine for lunch. On one occasion he was hearing the case against a man charged with attempting to indecently assault a little girl of nine.

Glowering at the defendant and his counsel, Mr Lowdon told the child to leave the witness box and sit on a chair next to his on which he had placed a large cushion. He repeated her whispered evidence in a stentorian voice, complimented her on her composure at the end of her story and then challenged the defending lawyer to cross-examine.

He did so, asking, 'Do you remember how the conversation between you and my client started?'

'Not really.'

'Did you begin by asking him something?'

'I might have done.'

'And do you remember what your question was?'
'Not really.'
'Didn't you ask him for a light for your cigarette?'
'Oh, yes, I did.'
'Get back into the witness box, you little hussy,' roared a disgusted Lowdon. 'Case dismissed.'

QUICK-THINKING

A busy magistrate was going through guilty pleas to various motoring offences, in every case rattling off a similar penalty: 'Fined £25 and licence endorsed.'

Suddenly the clerk objected: 'That last offence was non-payment of a TV licence.'

The magistrate hardly hesitated. 'Very well,' he snapped, 'in that case cancel the endorsement.'

PATIENT

A defendant appeared at Marlborough Street charged with disorderly conduct. She was deaf and dumb, as were the witnesses and all the spectators. When the magistrate asked if anybody could interpret for the accused, a woman raised her hand. Friends in the gallery gesticulated wildly. A long silence followed. It became clear that the interpreter was also deaf and dumb. Nobody in the court could understand sign language. As witnesses, friends, relatives, the interpreter and the accused all attempted to make themselves understood the courtroom was filled with wild gesticulations.

The magistrate, deciding it was hopeless to continue, discharged the defendant by smiling, shaking his head reprovingly, wagging his finger and pointing towards the door. As the defendant left the dock she gave a little dance of delight. The public cheered soundlessly. 'Silence in Court,' bawled the usher. But later he agreed he had never heard such a well-conducted case.

*   *

An equally silent defendant was Mr Mervyn Poncelet, of St Leonards, Sussex, who appeared before magistrates charged with walking naked down a main road. Maintaining a vow of silence he answered questions by holding up cards. When asked whether he was willing to speak in court, he held up two cards, one marked YES and the other NO. Told he would be bound over to keep the peace, he produced a third card which read I INTEND TO APPEAL. Informed he would go to prison for six months unless he agreed to be bound over, Mr Poncelet held up the card marked YES and left the court in silence.

As a Judge you Must . . .

TEMPER JUSTICE WITH COMMON SENSE

Michael Ward, of York, admitted he had been planning the murder of his spouse for over a year. Mr Justice Jupp placed him on probation for two years, explaining, 'You are a danger to no one except your wife.'

*   *

After pleading guilty to murdering her lover, Miss Lee Griffin of Orlando was sentenced to ten years' probation on condition she obtained a high-school diploma in Civics and attended church each Sunday.

*   *

Charged with libel against which he could offer no defence, John Cherry, editor and publisher of the *Seattle Times*, agreed to the judge's suggestion that the plaintiff, Mrs Diana Line, be allowed to pelt him with custard pies. Unable to find suitable pies, Mrs Line and her two sons, aged twelve and nine, flung chocolate creams at the editor – who stood on the steps of the newspaper office clad only in a bathing costume – until he was coated a uniform brown.

'I have seldom seen a plaintiff enjoy such satisfaction from a libel action,' remarked the judge.

* *

Overheard in an American courtroom:
JUDGE: I'm not going to sit here listening to this crap.
ATTORNEY: May I remind your honour this is election year.
JUDGE: Please continue.

BE HUMANE

After pleading guilty to stealing £5,000 Mr Thanes Nark Phong, head cashier in a Bangkok hotel, had his sentence of 865 years reduced to 576 years in recognition of his having helped the police.

BE WITHOUT PREJUDICE

A deputy circuit judge sitting at Croydon Crown Court was sentencing a West Indian youth for his ninth offence of pickpocketing. The proceedings had been strongly contested with numerous allegations of racial bias made against police and civilian complainants. Before passing a two-year jail sentence the Assistant Recorder addressed him thus:

'I want you to understand that I am here to perform a duty that the law requires. I must safeguard the public from activities of this kind. I do so blindly and impartially, and on the basis of the offence that you have committed in the context of your appalling record. I want you to understand that your racial origin and the scurrilous way in which you have tried to use racial bias as a defence have not influenced me in any way. Put Sambo down.'

BE DIGNIFIED

Asked if he thought it consistent with the dignity of his office to munch hamburgers and drink beer on the bench, District Judge John Simmons of Oklahoma explained that his working lunches helped speed up trials. When asked why he had stubbed out cigarettes on his tongue, aimed a revolver at District Attorney Habstich and, on the occasion of the Attorney's divorce, presented him with a large cake bearing a vulgar inscription in mauve icing sugar, Judge Simmons responded, 'I only did those things to liven up dull cases.'

*   *

Judge Leland Geiler's dismissal from the Californian bench has been urgently requested by court officials who disapprove of his using an electric dildo in place of his gavel.

HAVE A READY WIT

At the conclusion of a trial at Snaresbrook Crown Court, His Honour Judge Robinson sentenced the defendant, a burglar, to three years' imprisonment. As he was led from the dock the prisoner informed his Lordship he was a 'cunt'.

Ordering that he be brought back into the dock, Judge Robinson addressed him thus: 'You are going to be taken from this court and driven in a police van to Wandsworth prison. You will there be given a set of prison clothes and then locked in a small cell. You will be given an inedible meal and a cup of cold cocoa. Lights go out at 8.30 P.M. and you will then have eleven hours to look forward to slopping out tomorrow. I shall drive back to my comfortable home in my Mercedes motor car, where my adoring wife will greet me with an aperitif and leave me to relax with the newspaper in our living room while she prepares a delicious dinner which we shall enjoy together with an excellent bottle of wine. I shall then smoke a good cigar with my brandy and coffee, and a little later I shall retire to bed with my beautiful wife. Now which of us, would you say, was the cunt?'

* *

When sentencing an elderly and rather deaf sex offender the judge commented: 'This has been one of the most disgusting cases it has been my misfortune to hear in all my years on the bench and, despite your advanced years, I have no hesitation in passing a sentence of six years' imprisonment.'

Realizing that the old man had heard nothing of the judge's comments, a burly police sergeant informed him in a loud whisper, 'Judge says you're a dirty old bastard and you've got seven years.'

'Sergeant,' remarked the judge politely, 'whilst you have every right to paraphrase my sentence, I fear you have no powers to increase it.'

BE VERSATILE

The directors of a finance company involved in civil proceedings as plaintiffs seeking the return of monies they had loaned, reported Judge Williams for making bleating noises during the trial.

'Ba ba ba . . . that's what I say when I see defendants

being fleeced by greedy money-lenders,' said Judge Williams. 'By the way, I also do very good chicken noises, but I seldom use them in court.'

BE FIRM

Sending a rapist to jail for 1,500 years Judge Harvey Martin of Ohio explained, '500 years would be a slap on the wrist.'

*　　*

Polk County judge Franklin D. Westernholme returned after his luncheon adjournment to find that he was locked out of his court. After the efforts of the court ushers to gain him admittance had failed, Mr Herbert Furnace, a defence attorney, offered the services of his client, the safe-breaker Alan J. Larsen, who was due to appear before the judge that afternoon. Thanks to Larsen's skills, the court was able to resume a few minutes later. Following his guilty plea, the judge – after thanking Larsen for his help – sentenced him to ten years' imprisonment. He added, 'A man of your extensive criminal experience must appreciate that justice is blind.'

*　　*

After pleading guilty to more than 200 muggings in a New Jersey Court, defendant James Driver was surprised when Judge Nathan Heffer sprang from the bench, crossed the court and punched him in the face. Returning to the bench, he remarked, 'That's an example of honest police brutality.' The accused immediately asked the court to take a further nine stabbings into consideration.

BE FAIR

Judge Allen Daggett of Texas never passes sentence without keeping his Magnum pistol close at hand. He's carried a weapon ever since he was forced to leap from the bench to disarm a gun-toting witness. But he still maintains admirable judicial fairness in its use: 'I always give them the first shot,' he says, 'but boy, they had better not miss.'

*   *

Farmer Duff of Drogheda admitted his dog Sho-Sho had been driving the car when they were stopped by Constable Flynn. He explained that after losing his own licence he had taken out another in the collie's name.

'I know a good driver when I see one,' he commented, 'and Sho-Sho is one of the best.'

Judge D. Donleavy remarked, 'I once saw a talking horse on the television and it seemed perfectly normal to me. Case dismissed.'

BE AESTHETIC

'And what makes the heinous crime even more reprehensible,' remarked an Old Bailey judge sentencing a rapist, 'is that it took place under one of London's loveliest bridges.'

BE PRAGMATIC

After sentencing Linda Sue Jones to twenty years' imprisonment for attempted contract killings on her first two husbands in order to claim $600,000 insurance, the same judge married her for the third time to a Mr William Dobbs. 'It's a triumph of hope over experience,' commented the judge sadly.

*   *

Deciding to give a drunken tramp a last chance, the judge told him, 'Normally I would impose a custodial sentence on you. But on this occasion I will give you just one last chance to break this tragic habit. I will suspend your sentence on your promise never to touch a drop of drink again. You understand what I am saying.' The judge gazed sternly at the wretched meths drinker before him. 'No alcohol at all. Not even the teeniest, weeniest sherry before luncheon.'

*   *

Arrested while carrying a stolen automatic dispenser holding 250 packets of chewing gum, Samuel Curtis was sentenced by a Philadelphia judge to pay for and chew every piece. When the machine was empty of gum but full of money it was handed back to the owner and Curtis allowed to leave court.

*   *

A defendant appearing in a London Crown Court asked for an adjournment on the grounds that his wife was about to conceive. The judge, suggesting that he really meant his wife was about to give birth, added, 'I suppose in either event you had better be there.'

*   *

Arriving at court one-and-a-half hours late, Judge Stanley Kirk of Houston, Texas, directed the clerk to arraign him for contempt of court. After pleading guilty he fined himself $50, then announced, 'Bearing in mind this defendant's impeccable character and excellent record of public service, I feel on this occasion able to suspend the penalty.'

*   *

Hauled before the courts for making an obscene gesture at a High Court judge, the defendant explained he had mistaken him for the Mayor of Tees-side. The explanation was accepted and the man released.

BE A MAN OF THE WORLD

André Marck, who claimed to have slept with a woman but failed to notice that she had an artificial navel, was convicted of perjury by a court in Montpellier, France. 'A false belly button cannot be missed,' explained the judge.

*   *

The discovery that her husband was seeing another woman caused Mrs Betty Kilter to drag him through the garden by his hair, beat him with a rolling-pin, burn his shirts and stamp collection, flush away his gold cufflinks and order him to sleep in the car.

Mr Justice Camber determined that Mr Kilter's adultery was 'substantially worse than his wife's understandable response', but still granted him a divorce. Mrs Kilter denied her marriage had broken down.

*   *

Charged with murdering his second wife, Parisian Noël Carriou explained that he had killed his first for undercooking his steaks and his second, twelve years later, for overcooking them. Sentencing him to one year for manslaughter, the judge said, 'Good cooking is essential for a happy marriage.'

*   *

Dismissing a claim for wrongful dismissal brought by Mr Herbert Winkle, a fish gutter, the judge commented that one had to consider the expression 'fuck off' in the context of a job. While in certain occupations 'fuck off' might be interpreted as meaning immediate dismissal, on a fish dock the phrase meant little more than 'good morning'. He concluded that Mr Winkle had been overly hasty in seeking another job.

YOU NEED A PRACTICAL STREAK

Determined to demonstrate to a jury how handcuffs work, a judge brushed aside protests from the prosecuting counsel and quickly fettered himself.

'And that, members of the jury, is how it is done,' he explained. Then, turning to the counsel, he said, 'You may now release me.'

'That's what I was trying to explain, My Lord,' said the barrister. 'The police have not yet recovered the keys.'

DEAL FIRMLY WITH A JURY

Ordering a prospective juror to stand down, Judge Walter Brauer told a Californian court, 'From many years' experience I have every reason to believe that if this woman is permitted to take her place on the jury she will pay no attention to anything I say. She is my wife!'

*   *

Mr Jabez Teeweek failed in his attempt to have his conviction overturned by the Supreme Court of Santa Cruz, California. He argued the judge had put improper pressure on the jury to return a verdict when, after a retirement of three hours, he warned them that they would have to pay for their own lunches. The jury had brought in a guilty verdict two minutes later.

*   *

Mr AB, a lifelong prosecutor, finally achieved his ambition to sit as a deputy circuit judge at Woodford Crown Court. Appreciating that his chances of a full-time appointment would be immeasurably enhanced if he sided with the prosecution throughout the trial, he strove to demonstrate his even-handedness by affording every consideration to the jury. Throughout the trial he invited them to ask questions, at any stage, if a point was unclear to them. He explained that the proceedings were for their benefit, and they alone were the judges of fact. He then proceeded to sum up the case, reiterating every prosecution argument and ignoring the defence except for the odd derisory remark. He concluded by asking them, again, if prior to their retirement they had any questions.

'Only one,' said the foreman. 'We were just wondering why you are so appallingly biased?'

*   *

A trial for attempted murder in the Supreme Court of Manitoba was halted after nine days when a juror, Miss Aime Dunne, asked the judge to speak up a bit.

Enquiries revealed that Miss Dunne, who was completely deaf, was under the impression that she had been trying a divorce case. Further questioning revealed that another member of the jury spoke no English. Attending the courthouse to apply for a pistol permit he had been shown into the wrong waiting room. Told he was serving on a murder jury the man expressed great surprise. Finally it was discovered that a third jury member was both deaf and unable to speak English. The case was abandoned.

*   *

A farmer charged with having sex with his sheep admitted his intention but claimed all attempts at intercourse had ended in dismal failure. 'Do you expect the jury to believe you were in that field for three hours during which time you caught several sheep, but all escaped before anything occurred?' demanded prosecuting counsel incredulously. Before the accused could answer, a jury member commented loudly to his companion, 'Well, we all know that can happen.'

FOUR

Before the Law

COUNSEL: Have you any idea what your defence is going to be?

DEFENDANT: Well, I didn't do it, sir.

COUNSEL: Yes, well, er, I think we can afford to fill that out a little. It's not in itself a cast-iron defence.

DEFENDANT: Well, I didn't do it, sir! I didn't do it! And if I did it, may God strike me dead on the spot, sir!

COUNSEL: Well, we'll just give him a moment shall we?

Alan Bennett, *The Defending Counsel*

Although as a defendant you might expect a starring role, in practice you'll be little more than a bit player in the courtroom drama. Unless giving evidence your only lines may be a ringing 'not guilty' at the start and a plaintive 'so help me, I'm innocent' immediately before the final curtain. Other than that you will not be allowed to speak unless told to do so nor, indeed, perform any action which is not part of the carefully stage-managed presentation.

Should you be unfortunate enough to get cast in this role, here are some basic rules to ensure favourable reviews and short engagements.

DO – LOOK THE PART

It's terribly important to make a favourable impression on the audience. Preferably be white, middle class, well spoken – with a BBC accent – and dressed for a funeral. It helps to be a white-haired ex-serviceman with a limp, or similarly acceptable war wound, and several medals.

DO – ACT REMORSEFUL

It's what your audience expects and they don't take kindly to being disappointed. Take as your model the man charged with indecent exposure who entered stage left on crutches and sobbed on the witness stand. So spellbinding was his performance that, despite overwhelming evidence, he was unanimously acquitted.

DO – HAVE SUPPORTING PLAYERS

They should be attractive, sympathetic and prepared to give tearful evidence on your behalf. In one case the defendant's attractive wife cried on the witness stand and four of the jury sobbed with her. Such audience participation virtually guarantees a not-guilty verdict, and so it proved in this instance.

DON'T – HAM IT UP TOO MUCH

On trial for embezzlement, a female defendant wore a big cross around her neck, opened her Bible on the witness stand and took a large bottle of smelling salts from her bag. She came across as a pious old fraud and was found guilty, one suspects, for over acting as much as criminal conduct.

DON'T – APPEAR TOO SMART

Remember that like all stars, barristers and judges take grave exception to being upstaged by bit players.

DO – CREATE A SYMPATHETIC ROLE

Take as your inspiration the woman charged with
manslaughter who was attractive, modestly dressed,
claimed to have TB and wore a white mask throughout the trial (a nice touch this), had a loyal and likeable
husband; a good-looking twelve-year-old son; was
kind to animals and loving towards her own mother.
The judge was convinced of her guilt. The jury acquitted.

SHOW IMAGINATION

Applying successfully for a three-month adjournment
of his murder trial, Mr Popule Gig of Rue Nixon,
Port-au-Prince, explained his intention of using the
time to resurrect the victim whom he would then call
as a defence witness.

DON'T OVERDRAMATIZE A MINOR ROLE

During divorce proceedings in a Jacksonville, Florida,
court, Mr and Mrs Rudell Hickson drew guns and
started taking pot shots at each other from either end
of the chamber. Hearing the gunfire, Fred Lamp, a

witness in a nearby court, borrowed a pistol from the judge and shot them both dead.

*   *

Incensed by a magistrate's description of them as 'jobless yobbos', James and Henry Invite started leaping up and down in the dock. They abruptly vanished as the floor collapsed. During a short adjournment carpenters were ordered to cut holes in the front of the dock so that the prisoners could poke their heads through to watch the bench sentence them to six months.

AVOID TAKING TOO MANY ENCORES

Making his five hundredth appearance before a Leeds court on a charge of drunkenness, George Linstrum, seventy-six, said he had first been arrested in 1912. Two days later on his five hundred and first appearance he explained, 'I was celebrating my anniversary.'

BE PRAGMATIC

Summonsed to the District Court in Dallas to show cause why her Rotweiller dog, Byron, should not be destroyed after killing her four-week-old daughter, Mrs Amy Rognaldesen tearfully explained she could always have another baby but never replace Byron.

*   *

Not long after taking out an injunction to prevent her former husband, George, living in their bungalow, Mrs Doreen Tooting returned to find her home a pile of rubble. He had demolished it with a bulldozer. George Tooting said he would apply for the discharge or variation of the ouster injunction on the grounds that his wife no longer wished to live in the rubble and had gone back to mother. He, on the other hand, was quite happy to live alone amidst the debris.

Select a Plausible Explanation From These Well-tried Favourites

IT WAS ALL A MISTAKE

Apologizing for his savage attack on Mrs Maria Kouralis, Mr Eleftherious Saridis explained he had mistaken the victim for his wife.

*   *

Charged with causing more than £100,000 of damage to earth-moving equipment, rabbit-hunter Lewis Bedford of Adelaide offered this explanation to a South Australian court: 'While on a hunting trip, I accidentally bogged my van down in soft mud at the edge of a lake. To remove it I borrowed a tow truck from a local garage. Unfortunately this too became stuck. Going to a nearby construction site I took a twenty-ton bulldozer in the hope of removing both vehicles. Unfortunately the bulldozer also became bogged down. Desperate, I borrowed the only remaining vehicle on the site, an earth mover valued at £40,000, but this too became embedded in the mud. Sorry.'

*   *

Explaining how he came to knock professional wrestler Neil Goldie unconscious with his Mars Bar, Mr Jimmy Anders, a driver's assistant from Cumberland, explained he had flung it through the van window because he had toothache. 'I did not intend any harm,' he insisted.

*   *

Describing a journey which ended in charges of reckless driving, Mrs Alva Mays of Mule Creek, Texas, explained that it had all started with a telephone call from the police to say her sister had been hurt in a motor accident. Determined to be at her injured sister's bedside, Mrs Mays jumped into her car and, shortly after 9.00 A.M. entered the Santa Monica freeway.

'I attempted to negotiate the downtown Los Angeles interchange sixteen times,' she told the court, 'but finally gave up and spent the night in Bakersfield. During this time I received six traffic violations for either driving too fast or too slow. The next day started badly because I was trapped in dense fog on the Oceanside overpass for twelve hours. In all I travelled along nine different freeway systems during a journey which lasted three days, ten hours and seven minutes. It ended after I crashed through barriers at the start of an unfinished four-mile extension to the Garden Grove Freeway and drove into officials attending the ribbon-cutting ceremony.'

*   *

Charged with dangerous driving Mr Kenneth Graves told a Reading court that his blood alcohol level was only over the legal limit because he had eaten two large helpings of sherry trifle.

*   *

The fifteen members of the Stamford Scrabble Association had to abandon their competition when a torrent of water brought down the ceiling on them. Summonsed for criminal damage, Mr Thor Ocon, who gave his occupation as gentleman and lover, admitted breaking into the flat above the Scrabble Association headquarters to renew his association with Miss Leone Feldmann. When she refused to accommodate him, he stabbed her queen-sized water-bed in revenge.

*   *

Pleading guilty to gunning down Ms Fanny Finkle, aged seventy, Percy Watson, of Rochester, New York, also aged seventy, explained he had decided to murder his wife, Corrine, after a series of arguments. Watson, a retired army sergeant, opened fire as she emerged from the Mother's Day service at the Emmanuel Presbyterian church. 'I realized I had forgotten my glasses but by then it was too late to go home and collect them,' he explained. 'I shot the wrong woman by mistake.'

*   *

Charged with stealing a beer glass, Mr Peter Smith, a trainee aircraft controller who was arrested 200 yards from the airport hotel, Blackpool, explained that while walking home he had been approached by a man who complained that he had a glass stuck to his hand. 'I managed to unstick it, so he gave me the glass and beer as a reward. I am definitely not guilty.'

*   *

Denying a charge of criminal damage to a shop window, which police alleged he had head-butted into fragments, John Watson of Pinchbeck explained: 'While walking home I glimpsed my reflection in the window. Believing myself to be in danger of attack I decided to charge my assailant.'

*   *

Asked whether he had anything to say before sentence was passed, Mr Ahment Turker, aged seventy-two, of Yenisehir, explained that he murdered his wife on discovering she had not been a virgin when they married some forty-five years earlier.

*   *

Arrested on a charge of poaching, after being found in the middle of a trout stream dressed in a frogman's outfit, Mr George Silvers commented: 'This charge is ridiculous. I was taking my dog for a walk when it became frightened by a firework and jumped into the river. I was trying to rescue it when the water bailiffs arrived.' Asked to explain his rubber suit, flippers, mask and air bottles Mr Silver replied, 'I found them in the hall on my way out and just slipped into them.'

ANYHOW, IT WASN'T ME

Having ridden his bicycle through a red light, Mr Jeremy Eversholt was cautioned by Sergeant Bob Plant and asked why he was wearing a mauve skirt, cut-away blouse and black tights. 'Eversholt then sank his teeth into my forearm,' Sergeant Plant told the court. 'He held me with such tenacity that I was only able to restrain him with the help of up to forty passers-by.'

'The biting charge is nonsense,' protested Eversholt. 'I am a well-known West Country vegetarian.'

SO IT MUST HAVE BEEN SOMEONE ELSE

Giving evidence in the District Court at São Paulo, Señor William Nema claimed that his tortoise Coco had been responsible for bringing cannabis into his flat. 'Such cases are not unprecedented,' he claimed. 'I read recently of a rabbit called Bigorrilho who was found to have cocaine in its possession when coming through customs.' Dismissing his plea the magistrate pointed out that the rabbit had proved blameless. After the trial Señor Nema complained that Coco had also set fire to his flat as an act of revenge.

BUT IF IT WAS ME – I COULDN'T HELP MYSELF

Hong Kong stipendiary magistrate Mr Michael Hill dismissed the defence of 'automatism' put forward by Mr Lee Chung of Admiralty Avenue. Imposing a sentence of four months' imprisonment for indecent

assault, Mr Hill said, 'I am not persuaded by your argument that your thumb has suffered an irresistible pinching impulse since childhood.'

* *

Admitting crossing a double white line while passing a horse box, Mrs Dorothy Bradbury of Worksop explained she had been obliged to overtake because saliva from the cow it carried was obscuring her windscreen.

* *

Explaining how he had come to leave the road and crash through the hedge into the side of a bungalow, van driver Edward Milligan told the court, 'I was delivering hundreds of white mice to a laboratory and their heavy breathing fogged up my windscreen.'

*   *

Charged with exceeding the speed limit, meat pie salesman Mr Vincent Lally explained that steam from his cargo of black puddings had misted over the speedometer.

ANYHOW, THERE'S A REASONABLE EXPLANATION

Responding to a 999 call from Ms Edith Gosport, a traffic warden, PC Marcus Barnett arrived at Steyning's public lavatory to find Father Robert Champian, a church charity raffle organizer, kneeling against a party wall dividing the Ladies' and Gents' toilets.

'I first thought he must be praying,' Constable Barnett told the court. 'I then realized he was holding a hammer and chisel and that the floor was covered in plaster.' Father Champian explained he had only just purchased the tools and could not wait to get home before trying them out.

Admitting hiring a professional assassin to slay her husband, Iginia Petijean, of Liège, explained to the jury that she decided against divorce to avoid 'upsetting the children'.

*   *

Pleading guilty to a charge of speeding, Mr Christopher Gregory explained that he had travelled through a police speed check at ninety-eight mph while driving his mother-in-law home from Liverpool. 'I accelerated in surprise,' he said, 'when, after two and a half hours, she suddenly spoke to me.'

*   *

Charged with aiding and abetting a suicide, Mr Marvin Redland, a guitar salesman of Norfolk, Virginia, stated that he had always been interested in religious matters. 'I was having a quiet drink in the Cherokee Tavern when Dolly Weinberg, the barmaid, insisted she had been a canary in her previous incarnation. She went on to claim that in her next substantiation she would return as a buffalo. At this point I laughed in her face. Dolly appeared to lose her temper and seizing an automatic pistol kept behind the bar she shouted, "You'll see . . . I'll prove it!"

*   *

Pleading guilty to taking and driving away seven motor vehicles, and asking for several similar offences to be taken into consideration, Mr Simon Hervey, a poet, told Cork Crown Court that he had been protesting at the failure of local motorists to pick up hitch-hikers. This reluctance, Mr Hervey explained, even extended to those wearing St Christopher medallions. He asked the court to bear in mind that he had, on several occasions, been obliged to purchase petrol for the stolen cars, spending a total of more than £12. His application for bail was granted on the grounds that he had recently obtained employment reading evening prayers on the local radio station.

*   *

Arrested for traffic violations, Mr Nadras Ochoa, a student in Tampa, Florida, said he had driven backwards at fifty mph along the freeway because all the forward gears on his newly purchased truck had sheared. 'I was trying to get back to the garage before the twelve-hour warranty expired,' he explained.

*   *

Charged with possessing an offensive weapon, namely a chair leg studded with four-inch nails, Mr Nusraddeen Hussein told the court it was, in fact, a bat used in the Arabian beach sport of Ho-Ho. 'It is a game much like rounders, especially popular in Iran,' he said. Asked why he had the bat in his possession at night on Camber Sands, with no other potential players in the immediate vicinity, he explained, 'I was planning to walk into the sea in the hope of clubbing a few fish to death.'

* *

After a fracas involving several people at a continental-style level crossing, a court heard the following account of events from one of the witnesses:

'Being rather late for an appointment, I rode my moped to the front of a queue of vehicles waiting for the continental-style level crossing at Watts Hill. In so doing I rode ahead of Mr Blacker's horse and cart, whereupon the horse, Nancy, splattered my helmet and visor with saliva.

'I punched Nancy on the nose. She reared up, and spilled her load of scrap metal on to the car behind her belonging to a Mr Johnson.

'Mr Johnson got out of his car to remonstrate with Mr Blacker. We were joined by Mrs Dilly who tethered her Scottie dog, Oscar, to the bar of the level crossing whilst she recorded our particulars in a diary.'

Taking up the tale, British Rail signalman George Perkins described how, when the train passed and he raised the barrier, 'Oscar was left suspended from the bar and began choking. Realizing I must act speedily to prevent a potentially dangerous situation, I immediately dropped the bar, thereby saving Oscar's life and stunning two of the participants in the fracas, Mr Blacker and Mr Johnson.'

*   *

Before passing sentence on a teenager accused of stealing two bottles of vodka and a packet of cigarettes, magistrates considered a letter from the boy's headmaster. He suggested his pupil was suffering from stress associated with starring in the annual school play, *Jesus Christ, Superstar*, in which he played Christ.

*   *

Following his arrest for obstruction as he crawled around in the middle of the eight-lane highway which bypasses Lafayette, Indiana, Mr Heyman Cord told officers that he had been searching for his dentures which he had inadvertently flung from the car window together with a chicken leg he had been eating.

*   *

Mr David Bowen, who is blind, denied charges of drunken driving on the ground that his dog, Sir Anheuser Busch II, an Alaskan malamute, was assisting him. Bowen told the court Sir Anheuser Busch II barked to let him know the colour of approaching lights. When a well-informed magistrate objected on the ground that dogs are colour-blind, Bowen replied that his had been specially trained to identify the pattern of the changing lights.

*   *

A Greek nun, Sister Irene, appeared before the stipendiary magistrate at Buna, in Kenya, where she pleaded guilty to smuggling through customs 6,000 bees concealed under her habit. The nun explained that the bees were from Italy and produced a wax uniquely suitable for altar candles. Dr Isaac Kigatiia, of the Department of Agriculture, told the magistrate that European bees were known to suffer from various diseases whereas Kenyan bees experienced only diarrhoea.

*   *

Contesting a case brought under the Construction and Use regulations at Cleethorpes magistrates' court, Mr Ted Lichen claimed that if he was committing an offence in carrying his cat, Winkle, as a pillion passenger so also was a farmer on his way to market who had mice in his cargo, or 'a family motorist with a fly on his windscreen'.

*   *

Appearing in court on charges of driving without a horn, Mr Peter Harding of Congleton told the court, 'If I see anything coming I just shout. My voice is the equal of any horn.'

* *

Charged with attempting to smuggle half a pound of cannabis resin through Heathrow hidden under her hat, Miss Espenia Minott explained, 'I keep it there to ward off headaches.'

* *

When police raided the home of Jaap Van Dam, aged seventy-five, of Amsterdam they found more than 600 stolen bicycles crammed into three rooms. Mr Van Dam, a former champion cyclist, told the court, 'I have been interested in bicycles all my life.'

I WAS PROVOKED

Arrested on charges of attempting to murder a hang-glider pilot, Mr Frankie Thomas of Durban told the court that his intended victim had made an obscene gesture at his wife, who had been sitting naked on the garage roof enjoying a snack. 'They are always flying over our house,' he said. 'I have put up with it for years, but this was too much. I grabbed a machine-gun and let him have a burst.'

*   *

Theodore Duncan, of Oxford, broke windows, vandalized a telephone, smashed up a three-piece suite, hurled a TV and tape recorder into the street, tore out a bath and flung a wardrobe down the stairs. He told a court he was demonstrating his anger at 'the over-commercialization of Christmas'.

*   *

Describing how a fight had broken out in a fashionable Burnley nightspot, thirty-nine-year-old grandmother Norma Cummings explained she had been attempting to recite a poem – 'My Name is Diamond Lil' – to her girlfriend Lilly Twig. Upset by this, Lilly Twig punched her friend in the face.

'At this point I decided to remove my false teeth,' said Norma. 'As I did so I was given a karate chop which sent my teeth flying to the floor. While attempting to retrieve them from behind a radiator, I accidentally pulled off Lilly's jumper. At this she seemed to go crazy and the only way I could think of to calm her down was by using both fists.'

*   *

Tommy Hitchen, a railway worker who pleaded guilty to criminal damage at Whitley Bay magistrates' court, explained that his patience had been exhausted by attempting to take his own life. 'I had a few drinks and decided to walk into the sea,' he explained. 'It was so cold I had to give that up. So I returned home and wired up my easy chair and tried to electrocute myself. But I only blew all the fuses. Still in darkness, I tried to hang myself from the staircase, but the knot slipped and I fell heavily, spraining my ankle. I decided to go out and ring the Samaritans but their number was permanently engaged. This made me so angry I smashed up the phone box instead.'

*   *

Driven to distraction by the 'crowds of copulating couples making filthy noises all night', sixty-eight-year-old Mr Leonard Cracker rushed from his cottage near Lovers' Lane and attacked the nearest pair with his knobkerrie.

'We are not a loving couple at all,' protested one of the victims, Mr Donald Worse. 'We've been married twenty years and only returned to Lovers' Lane in the hope of rekindling our earlier passion.'

The Aberdeen sheriff court heard that he and his wife had received wounds which required twelve stitches. The under-sheriff, Mr McMister, warned Mr

Cracker that since this was his thirteenth offence he would have to consider confiscating the knobkerrie if it happened again.

* *

Pleading guilty to strangling his mother-in-law, Irene Tuck, Mr Frederick Dobson told the court he had been driven to murder because she refused to stop talking during the *Des O'Connor Show*.

* *

Charged with stabbing Miss Joan Naylor in the bottom with a pair of scissors, seventy-three-year-old Brenda South explained that, for more than three months, she had been watching *Jackanory* on a television in the window of a local television showroom.

'I have been shopping there for more than thirty years,' she told the court, 'and the set was placed in the window for the convenience of customers. Miss Naylor and her friend, who were at the front of the crowd, kept bobbing about and blocking my view, so I decided to teach her a lesson.'

* *

Mr Jacob Ginsley denied that he had set fire to his Skoda Octavia motor car for insurance purposes after it had broken down for the fourteenth time. 'I was

alone with the car on the hard shoulder and I thought I
would set fire to it as a distress beacon.' Ordering a
conditional discharge, the magistrate agreed that
there had been substantial provocation but suggested
that Mr Ginsley should 'brush up on the emergency
motorway regulations in case of breakdown'.

SURELY I'VE BEEN PUNISHED ENOUGH

After a row with his wife, Thomas Greenways of
Batford, near Sheffield, decided to take a few days'
holiday in London. Since he was travelling without a
ticket, the approach of an inspector caused him some
alarm. Slipping into the first class dining-car he borrowed a steward's crimson jacket. Emerging, he was
ordered to hurry up and get on with the lunches. From
then on, until his arrest some six weeks later, Mr
Greenways worked hard as a BR steward. Asking for
300 offences of theft of British Rail food to be taken
into consideration, he claimed his work more than
compensated for any food received.

*   *

Returning home after working for three years in Saudi
Arabia, Mr Desmond Gurney was enraged to find the
front door of his wife's home opened by a naked man.

Knocking him to the ground, he only gave up the attack when he discovered that the woman screaming from the top of the stairs was unfamiliar to him. 'I only realized later my wife had moved to America eighteen months before. I hope the court will also take into account the fact that I hadn't had a drink for three years.'

*   *

Accused of stealing a water cooler from a man who, he claimed, owed him money, Mr Lewis Matthew jumped bail of £25 and fled abroad. While working in Turkey he was arrested as a spy, kept in solitary confinement, brutalized, starved and so ill treated he went blind. Despite this handicap he escaped from prison and swam to freedom in Greece under fire from Turkish border guards. On returning home he was arrested and, after admitting selling the cooler for £3, fined £25.

BESIDES, IT'S SOCIETY THAT'S REALLY SICK

Arrested for selling pornographic photographs at Portsmouth central station, Mr John Cornell and Miss Phyllis Gladhand explained that, being short of money, they had snapped themselves in erotic positions using the automatic photo booth in the station forecourt. They had then attempted to sell these pictures to homeward-bound commuters.

'Although we had known one another for only ten minutes,' Mr Cornell told the court, 'I do not consider we have done anything wrong. Such photographs are now an accepted and popular form of entertainment.'

*   *

During the trial of Nigerian Adolf Potonas on a charge of having carnal knowledge of a chicken, evidence for the prosecution was given by Gladys Brittle, who described herself as a 'street entertainer'.

She told the court: 'I cannot understand what Mr Potonas can see in chickens, especially when women are so cheap around here. You can have one for just a few pence. He is a very handsome man and could have had me just for the asking. I would not have made any charge. His behaviour insults all the prostitutes of Nigeria and he should be brutally punished.'

THERE ARE MITIGATING CIRCUMSTANCES

Disputing the charge of driving with an excess of alcohol in his blood, Mr Gary Livingstone pointed out he had only one leg: 'It cannot be fair that through this disability alone, having drunk the same as a two-legged man, I should score a significantly higher reading.'

* *

After stopping an obviously overburdened Mini, New Jersey police found it contained twenty-seven passengers returning from holiday. 'It was not as bad as it seemed,' explained one of the passengers, 'because Eric, our driver, only has one arm.'

AND I'LL GO STRAIGHT FROM NOW ON

The Edinburgh sheriff court considered a written statement made by the defendant Edward Taylor in which he said that he had been glad that he was caught shop-lifting because the shock of his arrest would keep him from a life of crime. Mr Taylor appeared with his left leg in plaster having fallen off an office roof the previous night.

* *

As a defendant it's important to realize that . . .

ALL ADMISSIONS ARE RISKY

Bodmin Crown Court enjoys the reputation for trying many offenders charged with the commission of 'unnatural crimes' whose victims most commonly are sheep. An elderly shepherd facing a lengthy indictment for such crimes was troubled by a persistent cough to the extent that the clerk of the court could not understand his pleas.

The judge eventually interrupted: 'Have you ever tried sucking a Fisherman's Friend?'

The defendant replied, 'I'd rather not answer, My Lord. I think I'm in enough trouble already.'

*   *

Appearing at the Central Criminal Court in Brussels, M. Georges Le Maise admitted to the judge he had AIDS. The court immediately emptied, leaving M. Le Maise alone in the dock. Shouting from the corridor, a police inspector ordered him to go down to the courtyard and drive himself to Vaalasted Prison in a police van. He obediently did so. On arrival, however, the warders refused to allow him in. After consultation with the prison medical officer, the governor instructed Le Maise to drive the van to the main refuse depot and await further directions.

TRIALS TAKE TIME

The New York trial of Mr Hector Gusmann on drug-dealing charges has been proceeding slowly. The defendant speaks only Spanish and requires the services of an interpreter, Mrs Boniface Fiesta. Being blind she is accompanied by her guide dog, Big Boy, for whom the court regularly rises. A second interpreter is needed by one of the jurors who, three days into the trial, was found to be deaf and dumb.

THINGS CAN GO WRONG

Between committal and trial all five prosecution witnesses in an Old Bailey gangland trial disappeared. One had been dismembered, another shot dead, the third took a fatal overdose, the fourth died of drink and the fifth, a few minutes before a police escort arrived to take him to the court, left home never to be seen again. A police spokesman commented, 'We are satisfied there are no suspicious circumstances.'

EVEN HELPING THE COURT CAN PROVE RISKY

Summonsed to the Cape Town District Court where she was to appear as a witness, Miss Naomi Mallow found her way into the defendants' waiting room in error. Called into court, and overawed by the proceedings, she entered the dock and, after confusedly admitting eight shop-lifting offences, was jailed for two months.

DEMONSTRATIONS MAY BACKFIRE

'Having long hair gives me strength,' claimed Mr William Michin of New Jersey, while suing the Philadelphia Fire Department for wrongful dismissal. 'It is called the Samson Syndrome and poses no danger. Hair is self-extinguishing.' He then conducted an experiment to prove that waist-length locks would not impede his ability to fight fires and rescue people, by holding a lighter to the base of his hair. His head instantly caught alight. 'Pay no attention,' he shouted through the smoke and flames. 'It is due to my hairspray.'

AVOID TAKING THE LAW INTO YOUR OWN HANDS

Mr Estal Ziff has been sentenced to two-and-a-half years' imprisonment for false accounting, plus six months' consecutive for assault occasioning actual bodily harm. Branch manager of the National Bank, Pittsburg, Mr Ziff introduced a system of spanking overdrawn clients rather than charging them interest. These penalties were applied especially to young women, including six who had formed a publishing company and achieved an unauthorized debit balance of $180,000.

CIVIL ACTIONS CAN BE WORTHWHILE

Eric Edmonds, a twenty-three-year-old, twenty-two-stone man, is seeking $250,000 damages from a Virginia Beach hospital for allowing him near a refrigerator. In a drastic attempt to help him lose weight, his doctor had reduced the size of his stomach by implanting more than seventy stainless steel staples.

In his suit Edmonds complains that, two days later, after being 'allowed to raid the refrigerator' he ate so much his staples burst and it took emergency surgery to save his life. He claims the hospital were negligent for letting him anywhere near the fridge.

*   *

When Edith Spry, aged seventy-two, agreed to partner Jack Plowright, aged seventy, in the quickstep she hadn't realized how light on his feet he was. 'He just

whirled me around like I've never been whirled before,' she told a court after suing him for dancing without due care and attention. 'He was dancing at terrific speed. I was going to say "excuse me" because I was quite frightened.' Attempting a high-speed turn, they tumbled. Edith Spry claimed she was kicked in the leg and injured.

'It is alleged I danced boisterously,' said an irritated Mr Plowright. 'That is something absolutely alien to my nature.'

Dismissing Mrs Spry's claim, Mr Justice Boreham, aged seventy, remarked, 'I am terrified now. I shall never go near a ballroom again.'

* *

'I am definitely suing Good Foods Limited for damages and shock after finding a condom in my tub of cottage cheese,' says Mrs Filamina Linkag, aged eighty-seven. 'Imagine my humiliation when I opened the tub at a tea party and found myself spreading a contraceptive on to a slice of wholemeal bread.'

BUT DOMESTIC DISPUTES ARE MESSY

Giving evidence when his wife was facing charges of causing actual bodily harm, Mr Bill Penny of Man-

chester said he knew that their marriage was in difficulties after she had kicked away his invalid stick
causing him to fall to the floor. He explained that prior
to contracting a wasting disease it had been his habit to
give his wife a 'good kicking' several times a week. If
offered any food he disliked, Mr Penny continued, he
would throw the plate to the ground and trample it
into the carpet before giving her a 'good clouting'.
Since his illness none of this had been possible and, he
believed, his wife was no longer afraid of him.

Confirming her husband's story, Mrs Penny said
since he had lost weight her love for him had died. 'I
used to get a good kicking every Saturday night,' she
recalled. 'Now he is a mild man. It irritates me and
makes me nervous. The situation has become hopeless. I want a divorce.'

*   *

Before 1969 anyone who petitioned for divorce had to
disclose whether he, or she, had committed adultery.
This evidence was given in the form of a discretion
statement, placed in a sealed envelope and handed up
to the judge in the course of the hearing.

It was very rare to admit that more than one trans-
gression had taken place and normally only long after
the breakdown of the marriage and with the person

whom the petitioner hoped to marry once the divorce was granted.

A long-established firm of Eastbourne solicitors, more familiar with conveyancing and probate work, were asked by a wealthy family to prepare the papers for their daughter's divorce. Her disastrous marriage had lasted just four months. As she appeared to have difficulty in giving instructions for the discretion statement, the partner handling her case invited her to make notes so that he could draft it on her behalf.

A few days later she returned with a list of some fourteen names, together with appropriate *aides-mémoire*: the name of the hotel, party and even motor car where intercourse had taken place. The list concluded with 'MOB × 2'. Interpreting this to mean members of the Bar, and despite his fear that the firm's acute embarrassment at having to tender such a statement could only be increased by references to any members of the Bar they might instruct, the solicitor still advised that such persons must be named.

'But I can't even remember what they looked like,' the client explained. 'They were just two men on a boat!'

*   *

Three months after they were married Sandra Rugby stabbed her husband through the heart with a carving knife, the court was told. Defence counsel explained that, as he lay dying, Mr Rugby had said, 'I still love you . . . but this time you have gone too far.'

FIVE
Inside Jobs

LENNIE: Human weakness takes many forms.
Desire, greed, lust – we're all here for different
reasons, aren't we?

FLETCHER: With respect, Godber, we're all here
for the same reason – we got caught.

Dick Clement and Ian La Frenais, 'Poetic Justice', *Porridge*, BBC-tv

Your Part In the Prison Service

Not everybody wants the limelight. In crime, as in
show business, the smooth running of any production
depends on the backroom boys and girls. Of these the
most important are prison officers. Not only do they
ensure that essential players appear on stage on time,
they also have a hand in grooming many for their
demanding roles.

As a PO you'll have the satisfaction of watching
youngsters develop from minor roles as petty offenders to major villains landing leading parts in the most
important law courts of the land.

What does the job offer – apart from boredom, danger, and appalling conditions of employment? Well, for a start, there's variety. Many people think prison officers spend their time locking people up. Not so. They also unlock them. But not often.

With your charges behind bars for twenty-three hours a day, there is plenty of time for card games, smoking, drinking tea, planning industrial action and submitting enormous overtime claims – wages are currently around £500 per week.

Then there's job security. Shutting people away is a major growth industry. The UK now jails more people than any other European country apart from Turkey. And with the law and order lobby so powerful there's no need to worry about redundancy.

As to your place of work, there's only room here to deal with the main London theatres, plus an exceptional provincial one.

Pentonville – Best for filth. Years of accommodating those serving the shortest sentences, mainly drunks and dossers, obviously helped. But Pentonville has instituted two other measures to enhance its reputation: showers may be taken only once a week and all toiletries are removed from prisoners on reception.

Wandsworth – Best for violence. Plenty of seasoned

long-term prisoners, serving sentences for offences like armed robbery and a harsh regime are the main ingredients. Prisoners' families also participate in the daily fisticuffs. During a typical visit you will be able to enjoy major brawls as screws pounce on mums, dads, brothers, sisters, and girlfriends frantically passing drugs to inmates.

Wormwood Scrubs (The Scrubs) – Best for drugs. The exercise yard of C Wing has been favourably compared to Piccadilly Circus for the variety and quality of the illegal substances available, although prices are higher. For instance, heroin, with a street price of £60 a gram will cost closer to £120; one-eighth of an ounce of cannabis, street price around £12, about £20. Those with a heroin habit, so long as they have the money, need have no fear of suffering withdrawal symptoms. Better turn a blind eye to all this. The only thing which keeps most British prisons from erupting into violence is the fact that a majority of inmates spend much of their day stoned into oblivion.

Brixton – Best for nutters. F Wing, known as Fraggle Rock – after the popular children's television programme – is full of people who are mentally ill but haven't yet been 'nutted off' (hospitalized), plus assorted withdrawing junkies who were unfortunate enough not to get to The Scrubs. The suicide rate in Brixton is phenomenal. However, you need to be really determined since a single cell is obviously necessary to obtain the privacy needed to effect your own strangulation, and there is a long waiting list.

Holloway – Best for babies and buildings. It has a pleasant swimming pool, good educational classes, discussion groups, and lots of infants. A certain flexibility in sexual interests helps enormously.

Outside London there are a number of attractive low-security prisons. The most popular, with prisoners and screws alike, is North Eye in Sussex, considered by cognoscenti the Gleneagles of nicks. It has comfortable facilities and endless leisure activities – there is a nine-hole golf course at North Eye, jogging, light gardening, a well-equipped gym – and that's just for the inmates. All sorts of goodies are available to residents, not only drugs but bottles of booze, hampers of delicious food, mobile phones, even the prison uniforms are tailored to Savile Row standards. In every sense a high-class establishment. Although the standard of catering is not great, most sensible prisoners have their meals brought in from nearby restaurants, so you need not worry about complaints on that score. The only drawback is that you are forced to pass the day in the company of crooked solicitors, bent accountants and corrupt coppers, together with the occasional unfrocked vicar.

HAVE A DEEP RESPECT FOR HUMAN FEELINGS

The First World War machine-gun used to execute prisoners at Bangkok's Bang Khwang maximum security prison is being replaced by a more modern weapon. Explained Thavee Chusap, Director General of Thailand's correction department, 'Not being silenced, the old one disturbs prisoners at prayer.'

*　　*

E. Clifford Avery, serving life in a New Hampshire prison for the shot-gun slaying of a woman in 1973 is suing the authorities for failing to provide no smoking zones in dayrooms and washing facilities.

*　　*

Mark Lee Pollock, serving a seventeen- to forty-five-year sentence for burglary and passing dud cheques, is suing the prison authorities for cutting his hair. Pollock, thirty-one, says that for a follower of the religion of the Lakota American Indians, hair is sacred and should not be cut. By ordering his locks to be shorn,

Pollock charges Cincinnati prison officials with violating his constitutional rights.

HAVE AN INTEREST IN REHABILITATION

Elmer Copehhaver of Bowden prison, Alberta, pleaded guilty before the District Court to obtaining eighty-three credit cards in fifty-seven false names, all while serving a five-year sentence for fraud. Defending, Mr Harry Stanley explained, 'There was nothing dishonest about my client's behaviour in the conventional sense. He is preparing to take a degree in business administration and was seeking research material for a thesis on the use and abuse of credit cards.'

*　　　*

Point Hope prison, Alaska, holds the record for the most popular prison in penal history. Its reputation was made after two Eskimos, arrested by the local US marshal for minor violations, were so well fed and looked after they recommended it to all their friends. Soon Eskimos were breaking every law they could find just to be sent to jail. Before long the old prison became so overcrowded that a new one had to be built.

*　　　*

No less agreeable was Georgia's Tattnall 'model prison'. Here entertainments included petting parties, gambling tables and unlimited supplies of sex and drugs. Although thick walls and heavily guarded doors separated the male and female sections of the prison, a woman convict had only to ask for an electrician or plumber and a male prisoner would be sent to her cell.

'Remarkably, all the men were either electricians or plumbers,' said an investigating officer.

*   *

The Prison Ashram Project aims to help prisoners see their time inside as an opportunity for a 'considerable amount of meditation'. It has just been given the Best Prison Reform award.

*   *

After being released from Earlstoke prison, Devizes, Wilts, a group of old lags broke back in by cutting through the seventeen-foot high fence. They used their inside knowledge to make their way unnoticed to the nearby stores. After smashing a window they stole a £1,000 video camera. 'This was obviously the work of ex-prisoners,' said governor Roger Brandon. 'Unfortunately we don't know which ones.'

*   *

Having served four years for strangling a co-worker, Randy Don Landin was given employment by Honeywell, Inc. He has now been charged with shooting down another colleague, Kathleen Nesser, whom he stalked for weeks before slaying her with a shot-gun. 'We don't discriminate when it comes to hiring practice,' said a company spokesman.

*   *

After appearing before prisoners at a gala Christmas show in Wormwood Scrubs, pickpocket the Amazing Adam returned home minus his watch, wallet, braces, money belt and truss.

BE SUITABLY TRAINED

Señor Eluterio Sanches, one of Spain's most notorious criminals, serving a sentence of 1,022 years, has won the Benidorm song contest with his composition entitled 'I Wish'.

*   *

Puzzled by the sudden increase in costs of light bulbs at Collin County jail, Texas, prison officers kept a special watch on the cells. They quickly discovered the culprit. Convict Frank Reese, forty-four, was eating them. 'They are at their tastiest when still warm,' he said. Invited to perform on the local television station, Mr Reese ate fourteen bulbs and the sunglasses of the sheriff to whom he was handcuffed.

*   *

Much to the embarrassment of prison officers, Francesca Bellere, who is serving a sixteen-year sentence for terrorism in a maximum-security prison, has become pregnant. Defending themselves against attacks from government officials that such cases made nonsense of claims that their prisons were impregnable, a prison spokesman explained, 'We are convinced she was fructified while in the dock.'

ESCAPES CAN GIVE YOU A BAD PRESS

In July 1978, 124 convicts escaped from a Portuguese prison over a period of several days. Not only had officers failed to notice a significant fall in attendance at the nightly film shows – one movie was *The Great Escape* – they also overlooked spades, chisels, water hoses and electric drills concealed around the prison. Even large holes in the walls went undetected because they had been cunningly covered by posters.

'We knew 220 knives and a large amount of electric

cable had disappeared,' said a guard, 'but never got around to looking for them.'

The night before the majority of prisoners made their escape, a guard thought it strange that only thirteen out of the thirty-six prisoners on his block attended evening roll-call. But, he explained, it was normal for many to hide when the roll was being taken. 'They nearly always come back next day,' he added.

During the mass break out, the searchlights had turned out to be the guards' worst enemies. It proved impossible to turn them on the fleeing prisoners. Instead they shone straight into neighbouring watch towers, blinding the guards.

*　　*

After a hundred convicts escaped from Bomana jail in a mass break-out one Saturday night, an official for Papua's prison service admitted that 'security was not as tight as it should be'. He was able to report that one prisoner had, however, been recaptured. After stealing a car the man returned to the prison to pick up some of his friends who were due to escape later that evening. 'He was identified at the main gate,' said the official proudly, 'and immediately arrested.'

*　　*

When, in 1975, after months of back-breaking excavation, seventy-five prisoners from New Mexico's Soltillo jail emerged into daylight they found themselves in a nearby courtroom; the same court where most had received their original sentences.

*   *

Following his escape from prison, Mr Edward Davis was hunted by some 6,000 police for more than eight weeks. He was finally arrested in the public gallery of Bradford magistrates' court while attending the trial of his grandmother on a charge of drunken driving. Mr Davis was dressed as a woman and holding a two-year-old girl on his lap.

*   *

After being on the run for six years, oil rigger Ricky McKeand, twenty-nine, of Anahuac, Texas, has just started serving a five-year jail sentence for a shot-gun robbery carried out in 1978. He is suing the state for

failing to imprison him earlier. His suit charges the authorities with a lack of diligence in trying to find and arrest him.

* *

Accepting responsibility for the escape of Mr Robert Wilson who had been remanded in custody charged with the unlawful killing of Mr Henry Beaker, a spokesman for the Garda press office said, 'He is no more dangerous than any other murderer.'

Endpiece

Travelling to Bristol to deliver a lecture, James Pennent left his car for a few moments to answer a call of nature. Returning, he discovered not only that his pocket had been picked while he was in the lavatory but that the one tape in his car, a recording of his grandmother's funeral, had been stolen.

His lecture was entitled 'Law and Order – Is This The End?'